Desert Shadows: Uncovering the Underworld of Drug Cartels and Mafia Networks in the UAE

Robert Dobbs

DEDICATION

To the brave men and women in law enforcement and government agencies around the world who tirelessly work to protect our societies from the insidious threat of organized crime, and to the countless individuals and organizations dedicated to promoting awareness and education about the dangers of drug cartels and mafia groups. May your courage, resilience, and unwavering commitment to justice continue to inspire and uplift us all in the ongoing battle against the shadows that haunt our world.

CONTENTS

"I never lie to any man because I don't fear anyone.
The only time you lie is when you are afraid."
John Gotti

ACKNOWLEDGMENTS

First and foremost, I would like to express my deepest gratitude to my family, whose unwavering support and encouragement have been the cornerstone of my journey throughout the writing of this book. Your love and belief in me have been my source of strength and inspiration.

I am immensely grateful to my editor and wife, Ambreen, for her invaluable guidance, keen eye for detail, and endless patience in shaping this book into its final form. Her expertise and dedication have been instrumental in bringing this project to fruition.

A special acknowledgment goes to my colleagues and friends who have provided constructive feedback and words of encouragement throughout the writing process. Your support and camaraderie have been a constant source of motivation.

I would also like to express my gratitude to the librarians and archivists who assisted me in locating and accessing the necessary resources for my research. Their expertise and dedication have been invaluable in the completion of this work.

Lastly, I would like to acknowledge the countless individuals and organizations working tirelessly to combat organized crime and promote awareness about its dangers. Your efforts are vital in making our world a safer place, and I am honored to have had the opportunity to contribute to this important cause.

Thank you all for being a part of this journey.

PROLOGUE

Under the glimmering skyline of Dubai, a city that has emerged as a symbol of opulence and glamour, lies a dark and hidden world of international crime. The shimmering towers of glass and steel that dominate the landscape serve not only as a testament to the United Arab Emirates' (UAE) meteoric rise but also as a façade for an underworld of drug cartels and mafia networks operating within its borders.

In this gripping narrative, we delve deep into the intricate web of organized crime that has infiltrated the UAE, revealing a sinister side to the desert paradise that few dare to acknowledge. Desert Shadows: Uncovering the Underworld of Drug Cartels and Mafia Networks in the UAE exposes the complex connections and clandestine activities of criminal organizations from around the globe that have chosen this seemingly impenetrable haven as their base of operations.

The story begins with an exploration of the factors that have contributed to the UAE's vulnerability to infiltration by these shadowy organizations. The nation's strategic location at the crossroads of Europe, Asia, and Africa, coupled with its rapidly expanding economy and investment-friendly policies, has made it a magnet for individuals and groups seeking to launder money and conduct illicit activities. The country's sprawling free trade zones and lax corporate regulations have allowed criminal enterprises to establish shell companies and facilitate the flow of illicit proceeds with relative ease.

At the heart of this underworld lies a complex and diverse network of criminal organizations. From Indian and Pakistani crime syndicates to Italian mafia groups, the UAE has become a melting pot of criminal enterprise. Through a series of in-depth case studies, Desert Shadows brings to light the inner workings of these organizations, unveiling their intricate connections and the methods they employ to exploit the UAE's financial system.

One such example is the notorious Indian crime lord, Dawood Ibrahim, whose vast criminal empire spans multiple continents. Operating from his lavish safe haven in Karachi, Pakistan, Ibrahim has used the UAE as a conduit for his illicit activities, including drug trafficking, money laundering, and even the financing of terrorist organizations. His expansive network extends deep into the UAE's business and political spheres, enabling him to operate with relative impunity.

Similarly, the Italian mafia has found fertile ground in the UAE, using the country's well-developed infrastructure and financial system to expand their global operations. From drug trafficking to arms smuggling, these powerful criminal organizations have exploited the UAE's position as a global hub to further their nefarious interests.

But it is not only traditional organized crime groups that have found refuge in the UAE. The rise of cybercrime and the use of cryptocurrencies have provided new opportunities for criminal organizations to carry out their activities with even greater anonymity and efficiency. From online fraud and identity theft to sophisticated hacking operations, the digital underworld has become increasingly intertwined with the physical networks of organized crime in the UAE.

As the investigation unfolds, it becomes apparent that the UAE's efforts to combat these criminal networks have often fallen short of international standards. Despite recent attempts to strengthen its legal framework and enhance its law enforcement capabilities, the UAE continues to grapple with the challenges posed by its unique position as a global financial hub. The lack of international cooperation and the limited capacity of local authorities to detect and prosecute financial crimes have further exacerbated the problem.

However, amidst the shadows, there are also glimmers of hope. Desert Shadows examines the UAE's recent efforts to address these issues, from new legislation targeting money laundering and financial crime to increased cooperation with international partners. Through a combination of expert analysis and firsthand accounts, the book highlights the successes and failures of these initiatives, providing valuable insights into the ongoing struggle to combat organized crime in the UAE.

Desert Shadows: Uncovering the Underworld of Drug Cartels and Mafia Networks in the UAE serves as a stark reminder that beneath the glamorous surface of this desert metropolis lies a complex and often hidden world of crime and corruption. The book offers a rare glimpse into the secretive networks that operate in the shadows, far removed from the public eye, and the challenges faced by authorities in their attempts to dismantle these criminal enterprises.

As we journey through the dark underbelly of the UAE, we encounter a diverse cast of characters, from corrupt officials and high-ranking businessmen to street-level criminals and the victims caught in the crossfire. These personal stories shed light on the human cost of organized crime, illustrating the far-reaching consequences of these illicit activities on individuals, communities, and society as a whole.

The importance of the international community's role in addressing the global threat that organized crime poses is another important issue that Desert Shadows raises. As the UAE grapples with its own challenges, the book calls on the wider world to confront the reality of this growing menace and take collective action to combat the spread of criminal networks across borders.

Desert Shadows is a film that serves as a timely warning of the dangers that lie under the surface of our globalized society. In a world in which the borders between legality and criminality are becoming increasingly blurry and the tendrils of organized crime are stretching even farther, this film is particularly relevant. It is a narrative about money, power, and corruption, but it is also a story of perseverance, dedication, and the never-ending fight for justice in the face of adversity.

Not only does Desert Shadows: Uncovering the Underworld of Drug Cartels and Mafia Networks in the UAE expose the hidden world of organized crime in this desert paradise, but it also serves as a powerful call to action for individuals, governments, and institutions to join forces in the fight against this growing global threat. This is accomplished through gripping narratives and meticulous research. Together, we have the power to shed light on the darkness and strive for a future that is brighter and more secure for everyone.

Personal Experiences: A Glimpse into the Underworld

In my decade-long journey living in the UAE, I have had the unique opportunity to experience firsthand the presence and impact of drug cartels and mafia networks operating in this rapidly evolving nation. My personal experiences have given me a deeper understanding of the complexities and nuances of organized crime in the region, allowing me to provide an insider's perspective in this book, "Desert Shadows: Uncovering the Underworld of Drug Cartels and Mafia Networks in the UAE."

During my time in the UAE, I have had the chance to interact with various individuals connected to the Central Asian mafia operating in Dubai. While working for a company, I gradually discovered that my employer had ties to these mafia networks, which was a shocking revelation. This experience exposed me to the reality that organized crime can infiltrate even seemingly legitimate businesses, using them as a front for their illicit activities.

Additionally, I have had conversations with people from all walks of life who have felt the effects of organized crime in the UAE. From low-wage laborers to white-collar professionals, I have heard stories of exploitation, coercion, and violence at the hands of criminal organizations. These firsthand accounts underscore the pervasive reach of these groups and the detrimental impact they have on the lives of ordinary citizens.

In one particularly eye-opening encounter, I met a member of my extended family who had become entangled in the criminal underworld. This individual had fallen victim to the allure of easy money and the promise of a luxurious lifestyle, ultimately joining a smuggling and trafficking network. His tragic story is a testament to the power and influence that organized crime can wield over vulnerable individuals, ensnaring them in a dangerous web of criminality from which escape is often difficult, if not impossible.

These experiences have not only enriched my understanding of the subject matter discussed in this book but have also motivated me to continue my research and advocacy efforts to expose and combat the activities of drug cartels and mafia networks in the UAE. It is my hope that by shedding light on this dark and hidden world, I can contribute to the broader efforts to dismantle these criminal organizations and ensure a safer, more secure future for the UAE and its people.

As "Desert Shadows" explores the depths of organized crime in the UAE, it is essential to acknowledge that these networks are not mere abstract concepts or distant threats. They are very much present and active within our communities, affecting the lives of countless individuals. Through the stories and experiences shared in this book, I aim to raise awareness about the urgent need to confront and address the challenges posed by drug cartels and mafia networks, both in the UAE and beyond.

INTRODUCTION A.
THE EMERGENCE OF THE UAE AS A GLOBAL HUB

The United Arab Emirates (UAE) has seen a period of rapid development in recent decades, transforming itself into a worldwide center for commerce, banking, tourism, and innovation. The United Arab Emirates (UAE) has made the most of its exceptional location at the crossroads of East and West by making substantial investments in world-class infrastructure and adopting policies that are friendly to business. As a result, the UAE has attracted international corporations, investors, and skilled professionals from all over the world (Kanna, 2011).

The discovery of oil in the 1960s marked the beginning of the change in the UAE (Nereim & Algethami, 2018). This discovery provided the country with the financial resources necessary to invest in the nation's growth. After the United Arab Emirates (UAE) was established in 1971 as a federation of seven emirates, the country immediately set out on an ambitious path to diversify its economy and reduce its reliance on oil. This endeavor resulted in the formation of a variety of economic sectors such as banking, real estate, tourism, and renewable energy, all of which have drawn considerable foreign investment and contributed to the country's rapid growth (World Bank, 2019).

The United Arab Emirates' cosmopolitan cities, particularly Dubai and Abu Dhabi, have developed a reputation for being the pinnacle of luxury, modernism, and innovation. It has become a global magnet for visitors and expats seeking a high quality of life and exciting professional prospects due to the nation's famous buildings, state-of-the-art airports, and cutting-edge technology (Davidson, 2008). The United Arab Emirates has also established itself as a significant participant in international diplomacy and a generous provider of overseas assistance, thereby improving the country's standing in the international community (UAE Ministry of Foreign Affairs, 2021).

However, along with the numerous successes and accolades, the United Arab Emirates' rapid rise as a global hub has also brought with it a darker side. This is despite the fact that the UAE is a global hub. The United Arab Emirates (UAE) has become an attractive destination for criminal networks that are looking to take advantage of its advantageous location, advanced infrastructure, and ease of doing business (Reuter, 2020). These are the same features that have attracted legitimate businesses and investors to the UAE. Its strategic location, advanced infrastructure, and ease of doing business are among the features that have made the UAE an attractive destination.

In the book "Desert Shadows: Uncovering the Underworld of Drug Cartels and Mafia Networks in the UAE," we dig into the intricate and sometimes hidden world of organized crime in the UAE. We investigate its origins, expansion, and the effect it has on the society and economy of the nation. This book seeks to shed light on the challenges faced by the country in its ongoing battle against the criminal underworld and the urgent need for collaborative efforts to address this growing threat. It does so by examining the multifaceted connections between drug cartels and mafia groups that operate in the UAE.

Dubai, known for its stunning architecture, luxurious lifestyle, and world-class attractions, has undoubtedly made a name for itself as a global hub for tourism, business, and innovation. However, behind the glitz and glamour of the city lies a darker side, where organized crime, human rights abuses, and environmental concerns persist. This dark side of Dubai raises questions about the sustainability and ethics of its rapid development.

1. **Organized Crime:** The strategic location of Dubai, along with its business-friendly environment and advanced infrastructure, has attracted not only legitimate enterprises but also criminal networks. These organizations engage in drug trafficking, money laundering, human trafficking, and cybercrime, among other illicit activities (Shelley, 2014). As a result, Dubai has become a key transit point for the trafficking of narcotics, weapons, and people (UNODC,

2016). The presence of these criminal networks poses a significant challenge to the city's law enforcement and undermines its reputation as a safe and secure destination.

In recent years, the United Arab Emirates (UAE), particularly Dubai, has become an attractive destination for organized crime groups seeking a safe haven to conduct their illicit activities. The brutal Irish gang Daniel Kinahan leads is one such group that has established a base of operations in the opulent desert city (ICIJ, 2022).

The International Consortium of Investigative Journalists (ICIJ) published a detailed report in April 2022, outlining the various activities and operations of the Kinahan gang in Dubai. The report highlights how the gang's leader, Daniel Kinahan, managed to establish a strong foothold in the city despite being on the radar of international law enforcement agencies (ICIJ, 2022).

Dubai's lax investment laws, lack of stringent anti-money laundering regulations, and overall environment of secrecy have made it an ideal location for organized crime groups like the Kinahan gang. The ICIJ report states that the gang has used the city as a base to expand its global drug trafficking empire, which spans across Europe, Africa, and the Americas (ICIJ, 2022).

Furthermore, the report emphasizes that the Kinahan gang's presence in Dubai has not gone unnoticed by the White House. The Biden administration has reportedly been closely monitoring the activities of the gang and has expressed concerns about the UAE's inability or unwillingness to tackle the issue of organized crime within its borders (ICIJ, 2022).

The ICIJ report cites several sources, including a former high-ranking U.S. law enforcement official who claims that the Kinahan gang's operations in Dubai have put the UAE on the radar of the U.S. government. The official stated that the Biden administration is considering the possibility of imposing sanctions on the UAE if it fails to take appropriate action against the gang and its activities (ICIJ, 2022).

In response to the growing concerns over organized crime in the UAE, the country has taken some steps to strengthen its anti-money laundering and counter-terrorism financing regulations. However, critics argue that these efforts have not gone far enough and that the UAE needs to take more robust measures to combat the presence of criminal organizations like the Kinahan gang (ICIJ, 2022).

The ruthless Irish gang's presence in Dubai under the leadership of Daniel Kinahan has brought attention to the difficulties the UAE is having in addressing the problem of organized crime within its borders. As international pressure mounts, it remains to be seen whether the UAE will take the necessary steps to tackle this growing problem effectively and avoid potential repercussions from the international community.

2. **Human Rights Abuse:** Millions of migrant workers' labor has fueled Dubai's rapid growth, but they frequently endure abusive working conditions and other forms of human rights abuse. Many workers are lured to the city with promises of high wages and good living conditions, only to find themselves trapped in a cycle of debt and exploitation (Human Rights Watch, 2006). Some are forced to work long hours in extreme heat without adequate safety measures, while others live in overcrowded, unsanitary accommodations. The UAE government has taken steps to improve labor conditions, but progress remains slow, and abuses continue to be reported.

   In November 2021, the United Arab Emirates (UAE) made a bid for the presidency of the International Criminal Police Organization (INTERPOL), with Major General Ahmed Naser Al Raisi as the candidate (Stirling, 2021). However, this moves sparked concerns among human rights activists and organizations due to Al Raisi's alleged involvement in human rights abuses in the UAE.

Radha Stirling, founder and CEO of Detained in Dubai and IPEX Reform, released a statement expressing concern about Al Raisi's bid for INTERPOL's presidency (Stirling, 2021). According to Stirling, Al Raisi has been implicated in multiple cases of human rights abuses, including arbitrary detention, torture, and suppression of freedom of speech in the UAE (Stirling, 2021).

Stirling also highlighted the UAE's misuse of INTERPOL's Red Notice system, which is designed to facilitate the arrest and extradition of fugitives. In recent years, the UAE has been accused of using the system to target political dissidents, human rights activists, and debt defaulters, thereby turning INTERPOL into a tool for political persecution and human rights violations (Stirling, 2021).

Critics argue that allowing Al Raisi to assume the presidency of INTERPOL would further undermine the organization's credibility and integrity. They contend that his appointment would enable the UAE to continue exploiting INTERPOL's resources for its political agenda rather than focusing on international cooperation in fighting crime and terrorism (Stirling, 2021).

Despite the concerns raised by human rights activists and organizations, Al Raisi was elected as Interpol's president in November 2021. His appointment has been met with skepticism and apprehension from various stakeholders, who worry that it may lead to further human rights abuses and misuse of INTERPOL's mechanisms (BBC, 2021).

The UAE's bid for INTERPOL's presidency with Major General Ahmed Naser Al Raisi as the candidate has raised serious concerns about the country's commitment to human rights and the potential for abuse of INTERPOL's resources. As Al Raisi assumes his role as INTERPOL's president, it remains to be seen whether the organization will maintain its integrity and commitment to international cooperation in the fight against crime and terrorism.

3. **Environmental Concerns:** The rapid development of Dubai has also taken a toll on the environment. The city's construction boom, reliance on desalination, and high consumption of resources contribute to significant environmental challenges, such as water scarcity, air pollution, and habitat destruction (Gardner, 2009). Additionally, Dubai's artificial islands, such as the Palm Jumeirah, have been linked to coastal erosion, loss of marine life, and long-term ecological damage (The Guardian, 2009). These issues raise concerns about the sustainability of Dubai's growth and its ability to balance economic development with environmental protection.

The rapid development and urbanization of the United Arab Emirates (UAE) have brought with them significant environmental challenges, particularly in relation to water management. In a region where water is already scarce, the growing demand for this vital resource has led to increased pressure on limited supplies (MEI, 2021). This section will discuss the key water issues facing the UAE and the consequences of rapid expansion on the country's environment.

Overreliance on desalination: With limited natural freshwater resources, the UAE heavily relies on desalination to meet its water needs. While this process has provided the country with a steady supply of potable water, it has also led to a range of environmental problems. Desalination plants are energy-intensive, contributing to the UAE's high carbon emissions and exacerbating climate change (MEI, 2021). Additionally, the discharge of highly concentrated brine from desalination plants has a detrimental impact on marine ecosystems.

Agricultural water use: Agriculture is a significant consumer of water in the UAE, accounting for approximately 80% of the country's total water consumption (MEI, 2021). However, the majority of agricultural practices in the region are water-intensive and inefficient, contributing to the depletion of groundwater resources. Moreover, the cultivation of water-intensive crops, such as Rhodes grass, has placed further strain on the country's limited water supplies.

Groundwater depletion: The UAE's rapid expansion and increased water demand have led to the over-extraction of groundwater, resulting in the depletion of this finite resource. According to the Middle East Institute (2021), the UAE's groundwater levels have dropped by more than 60% over the past three decades. This depletion not only threatens the country's long-term water security but also contributes to land subsidence and soil salinization.

Wastewater management: The UAE's rapid urbanization has resulted in increased volumes of wastewater, which requires proper treatment and disposal to prevent pollution and contamination of water sources. However, the country's wastewater treatment infrastructure has not kept pace with the rapid growth in population and urban development, leading to environmental and public health risks (MEI, 2021).

The UAE's rapid expansion has brought with it a range of environmental challenges related to water management. The overreliance on desalination, inefficient agricultural practices, depletion of groundwater resources, and inadequate wastewater management infrastructure all contribute to the pressing need for action to address the country's water issues. To ensure long-term water security and sustainable development, the UAE must invest in more efficient water management practices, innovative technologies, and the development of a comprehensive water strategy.

4. **Wealth Inequality:** Dubai is known for its opulent lifestyle and displays of wealth, but beneath the surface, there is a

stark divide between the rich and the poor. The city's rapid growth has led to rising income inequality, with many low-wage workers struggling to make ends meet in the face of skyrocketing living costs (The Economist, 2018). This wealth disparity highlights the need for more inclusive and equitable development policies in Dubai.

The United Arab Emirates (UAE) is a country often associated with immense wealth and luxury. While it is true that the nation has experienced rapid economic growth and development, this wealth has not been distributed evenly among the population. Wealth inequality is a growing concern in the UAE, with a significant divide between the affluent and those living in poverty (The Borgen Project, 2020). This section will explore the causes and consequences of wealth inequality in the UAE and the measures that need to be taken to address this issue.

Migrant worker population: The UAE has a large migrant worker population, accounting for approximately 90% of the country's workforce (The Borgen Project, 2020). Many of these workers are employed in low-wage sectors, such as construction and domestic services, and often face poor working and living conditions. The low wages and lack of social protection for migrant workers contribute to the wealth gap in the UAE.

Limited social safety nets: The UAE's social safety net is primarily focused on its citizen population, with limited support available for non-nationals. Migrant workers, who make up the majority of the UAE's population, often do not have access to the same benefits and protections as Emirati citizens (The Borgen Project, 2020). This lack of assistance makes the wealth inequality migrant workers experience worse.

Education disparities: In the UAE, there are significant disparities in educational opportunities and outcomes between different segments of the population. While Emirati citizens generally have access to quality education, many migrant workers and their families face barriers to accessing education, limiting their opportunities for social mobility and contributing to wealth inequality (The Borgen Project, 2020).

Economic diversification: The UAE's economy is heavily dependent on oil revenues, which are subject to fluctuations in global markets. As the country seeks to diversify its economy and reduce its reliance on oil, there is a need to ensure that the benefits of economic growth are distributed more equitably across the population (The Borgen Project, 2020).

Addressing wealth inequality in the UAE requires a multifaceted approach that includes improving working conditions and wages for migrant workers, expanding social safety nets to cover non-nationals, and ensuring equal access to education for all residents. Moreover, as the UAE diversifies its economy, it is essential to prioritize inclusive growth that benefits all segments of society.

The UAE can work to create a more inclusive and equitable society by addressing wealth inequality, ensuring that all citizens share in the advantages of the nation's growth and development.

Dubai's Legal System: A Challenge for Foreign Investors and Expatriates

Dubai has emerged as a global hub for trade, finance, and tourism in recent years, attracting foreign investors and expatriates from around the world. However, despite its rapid development and modern image, Dubai's legal system has been a source of concern for many who have faced difficulties navigating its complex and sometimes opaque procedures. The case of Indian businessman Manmohan Singh is one such example that highlights the challenges faced by foreign investors and expatriates in Dubai (Gupta, 2003).

Singh, who had established a successful business in Dubai, found himself in a precarious situation when his local partner accused him of fraud and embezzlement. Singh was arrested, detained without charge, and faced the prospect of losing his entire investment in Dubai. According to the report by Gupta (2003), Singh's ordeal was not an isolated incident but rather an example of the broader challenges faced by foreign investors and expatriates in Dubai.

One of the main issues faced by foreign investors and expatriates in Dubai is the lack of transparency in the legal system, which can lead to arbitrary decisions and prolonged legal battles. In many cases, the laws and regulations governing business and investment in Dubai are not clearly defined or readily available, making it difficult for foreign investors to understand their rights and obligations (Gupta, 2003). This lack of transparency can be particularly problematic when disputes arise between foreign investors and their local partners, as the legal system tends to favor Emirati nationals in such cases.

Moreover, the legal system in Dubai has been criticized for its slow and bureaucratic processes, which can result in lengthy delays in the resolution of disputes. In some instances, foreign investors and expatriates have found themselves trapped in legal limbo for years, unable to leave the country or access their assets due to ongoing legal proceedings (Gupta, 2003). These delays can be financially and emotionally devastating for those involved, causing significant hardship and stress.

The challenges faced by foreign investors and expatriates in Dubai's legal system underscore the need for greater transparency, efficiency, and fairness in the administration of justice. While Dubai has made significant strides in its economic development, its legal system has not kept pace with these changes, creating barriers for foreign investors and expatriates seeking to do business in the emirate (Gupta, 2003).

In conclusion, Dubai's meteoric rise to prominence on the global stage as a center for business, tourism, and innovation is undoubtedly remarkable. The city has become synonymous with opulence, luxury, and architectural marvels, attracting millions of visitors and investors from around the world. However, beneath the glittering facade, there exists a darker side to Dubai, marked by organized crime, human rights abuses, environmental concerns, and wealth inequality. Addressing these pressing issues is not only essential for the long-term sustainability and stability of Dubai but also for preserving its reputation as a leading global city.

Organized crime networks, both local and international, have found a haven in Dubai to conduct their illicit activities, such as money laundering, drug trafficking, and human trafficking. Tackling these criminal networks requires a multi-pronged approach that includes strengthening legal frameworks, enhancing law enforcement capacity, fostering international cooperation, and investing in cybersecurity measures. By doing so, Dubai can send a clear message that it will not tolerate criminal activities and will work relentlessly to protect its citizens and visitors from the dangers posed by organized crime.

Human rights abuses in Dubai, particularly concerning the treatment of migrant workers, who make up the majority of the city's population, must also be addressed. Ensuring fair wages, decent working conditions, and access to essential services for all residents, regardless of their nationality or status, will promote social cohesion and demonstrate Dubai's commitment to upholding human rights principles. Additionally, addressing allegations of human rights abuses within the UAE's law enforcement and criminal justice systems will help enhance transparency and accountability.

Environmental concerns, such as water scarcity and pollution, pose significant challenges for Dubai, given its rapid urbanization and population growth. The city must adopt sustainable development practices and invest in innovative technologies to minimize its ecological footprint and preserve its natural resources for future generations. By prioritizing environmental sustainability, Dubai can set an example for other cities in the region and around the world to follow.

Lastly, wealth inequality in Dubai demands urgent attention, as it can lead to social unrest and undermine the city's social fabric. Ensuring equitable access to education, healthcare, and social safety nets for all residents, regardless of their nationality or socio-economic status, will help bridge the gap between the rich and the poor. Inclusive growth policies that prioritize the well-being and development of all segments of society will contribute to greater social harmony and overall prosperity.

In summary, addressing the darker aspects of Dubai, including organized crime, human rights abuses, environmental issues, and wealth inequality, is crucial for the city's long-term success and reputation. By confronting these challenges head-on and adopting proactive measures to mitigate their impacts, Dubai can solidify its position as a global leader in innovation, sustainability, and social progress, ensuring a brighter future for all its residents and visitors.

INTRODUCTION B.
OVERVIEW OF DRUG CARTELS AND MAFIA

For a very long time, organized crime has been a problem on a worldwide scale. Drug cartels and mafia organizations have for a long time operated in a variety of nations, taking advantage of lax governance, corruption, and socio-economic imbalances in order to further their illicit operations (Shelley, 2014). Mafia groups engage in a wider variety of illegal operations than drug cartels do, including extortion, money laundering, human trafficking, and weapon smuggling (UNODC, 2020). Drug cartels' primary concentration is on the manufacturing, transportation, and distribution of drugs.

Drug cartels and mafia organizations are notorious for their complex organizational systems, which allow them to carry out their illicit business in an effective manner and elude detection by the authorities. These criminal organizations frequently exhibit a great degree of flexibility, resilience, and ruthlessness in their pursuit of new possibilities to grow their businesses and safeguard their interests (Glenny, 2008). This is due to the fact that they are always looking for ways to broaden their scope of operations and safeguard their own interests. They are able to bribe public officials, infiltrate legitimate enterprises, and exert a substantial amount of influence over the areas in which they operate because of the enormous earnings made from their illegal operations (UNODC, 2020).

According to Reuter (2020), the presence of drug cartels and mafia organizations in the United Arab Emirates (UAE) may be linked to a number of circumstances, some of which include the country's strategic position, increasing wealth, and diversified population. As a result of the United Arab Emirates's emergence as a worldwide center, it has unwittingly offered a fertile ground for criminal networks to establish their presence, develop alliances, and abuse the nation's resources for the sake of furthering their own nefarious goals (Davidson, 2008).

In the next chapters, we will investigate the growth of organized crime in the UAE and the intricate relationship that exists between the many drug cartels and mafia groups that operate within the country's boundaries. We want to create a thorough awareness of the problems faced by these criminal enterprises and the essential actions to confront this rising threat by conducting an in-depth investigation of their activities, networks, and influence on the UAE's society and economy. This will allow us to achieve our goal of providing a full grasp of the issues.

In addition to this, we will talk about the United Arab Emirates' response to organized crime, which will include law enforcement measures, international collaboration, as well as preventative and public awareness campaigns (U.S. Department of State, 2020). We intend to contribute to the continuing conversation about how the United Arab Emirates (UAE) may best protect its security, wealth, and worldwide reputation in the face of the expanding danger posed by organized crime by evaluating the efficacy of these efforts and investigating potential solutions. This will be accomplished through the exploration of potential solutions.

As we delve deeper into the world of "Desert Shadows," it is essential to keep in mind that the purpose of this book is not to cast a negative light on the United Arab Emirates or minimize the country's many achievements. Rather than that, the purpose of this report is to shed light on a vital issue that deserves attention and joint action in order to assure the continued growth and prosperity of this magnificent nation.

Organized crime in Dubai has been known to involve a complex web of drug cartels and mafia groups, with members from various regions of the world. Although it is difficult to provide a comprehensive list of all the individuals involved, this section will discuss some of the key players and their activities in the city.

1. South Asian Cartels and Syndicates

Dubai has seen the presence of South Asian drug cartels and crime syndicates, particularly from Pakistan and India. These groups have established drug trafficking networks through which they smuggle narcotics, such as heroin and synthetic drugs, from their home countries into the UAE (UNODC, 2016). These cartels are also known to collaborate with local criminals and use the city as a transit point for drug shipments to other countries, including those in Europe and Africa (Europol, 2017).

In recent years, the United Arab Emirates (UAE), particularly Dubai, has become a hub for South Asian crime syndicates, which have been attracted by the city's rapid development, lax regulations, and strategic location (Gangarosa, 2014). The presence of these criminal organizations in Dubai has raised concerns about the city's ability to combat organized crime and maintain its reputation as a safe and attractive destination for international investors and tourists.

One of the most notorious South Asian crime syndicates operating in the UAE is the D-Company, led by Dawood Ibrahim, an Indian underworld figure who has been designated as a global terrorist by the United States (Gangarosa, 2014). The D-Company is involved in a wide range of criminal activities, including drug trafficking, arms smuggling, counterfeiting, and money laundering, with operations extending across South Asia, the Middle East, and Africa (Gangarosa, 2014). Dubai's strategic location at the crossroads of Asia, Africa, and Europe makes it an ideal base for the D-Company to coordinate its transnational criminal enterprises (Gangarosa, 2014).

Pakistani crime syndicates also have a significant presence in the UAE, with some reports suggesting that they are involved in drug trafficking, human trafficking, and organized prostitution (Gangarosa, 2014). The porous borders between Pakistan and Afghanistan, coupled with Dubai's status as a global transportation hub, make it relatively easy for these criminal organizations to smuggle narcotics and other illicit goods into the city (Gangarosa, 2014).

In February 2003, Dubai arrested and released a number of high-profile organized criminals linked to international terrorism, despite Interpol's red corner notices against many of them and India's recent handover of a list of these criminals to the UAE (Chaudhary, 2003).

According to initial reports, 26 members of the renowned Dawood Ibrahim gang, known as the "D-Company," were arrested in Dubai, including two of the gang leader's brothers, Noora (Noorul Haque) and Mustaqim, who are accused of the 1993 Bombay Blasts, a series of explosions in commercial centers that killed 257 people and injured 713 (Chaudhary, 2003).

All those detained in the current incident were freed with instructions to "leave the country immediately." It was unclear why Dubai took rapid action against these gang-lords and their cadres, as the main goal was to avert a slaughter in Dubai. On January 19, 2003, one of Dawood Ibrahim's lieutenants, Sharad Shetty, was killed at the India Club in the city in a revenge killing ordered by Chotta Rajan (Chaudhary, 2003).

The presence of South Asian crime syndicates in the UAE has raised concerns about the city's ability to effectively combat organized crime, particularly in the areas of law enforcement and judicial cooperation. While the UAE has made some efforts to strengthen its legal framework and enhance its law enforcement capacity, critics argue that more needs to be done to ensure that the country's institutions are equipped to deal with the growing threat posed by transnational criminal organizations (Gangarosa, 2014).

In order to effectively address the issue of South Asian crime syndicates operating in the UAE, the government must adopt a multi-pronged approach that includes enhancing its legal framework, bolstering its law enforcement capacity, fostering international cooperation, and raising public awareness about the dangers posed by organized crime (Gangarosa, 2014). Additionally, the UAE should work closely with regional partners, such as India and Pakistan, to share intelligence and coordinate efforts to dismantle criminal networks operating across national borders.

The presence of South Asian crime syndicates in the UAE, particularly in Dubai, poses a significant challenge to the city's security and reputation as a safe and attractive destination for international investors and tourists. Addressing this issue will require concerted efforts on the part of the UAE government and its regional and international partners to strengthen legal frameworks, enhance law enforcement capacity, and promote cooperation in the fight against transnational organized crime.

2. Russian and Eastern European Mafias

Organized crime groups from Russia and Eastern Europe have also been active in Dubai, engaging in various illicit activities, such as money laundering, cybercrime, and human trafficking (Shelley, 2014). These groups often exploit the UAE's business-friendly environment and its advanced financial and real estate sectors to launder the proceeds of their criminal activities, invest in legitimate businesses, and maintain a low profile (Hutchings & Guala, 2017).

In recent years, the United Arab Emirates (UAE), particularly Dubai, has emerged as a significant hub for Russian and Eastern European mafias. These criminal organizations have been drawn to the city due to its strategic location, rapid development, and relatively lax regulations (Lazarević, 2018). The presence of Russian and Eastern European mafias in the UAE has raised concerns about the city's ability to combat organized crime and maintain its reputation as a safe and attractive destination for international investors and tourists.

Russian organized crime groups, such as the Solntsevskaya Bratva and the Tambov Gang, have been known to operate in Dubai, engaging in a range of criminal activities, including drug trafficking, arms smuggling, money laundering, and extortion (Lazarević, 2018). In some cases, these groups have collaborated with local Emirati criminal networks to carry out their illicit activities, thereby expanding their reach and influence in the region (Lazarević, 2018).

Similarly, Eastern European criminal organizations, including Serbian, Albanian, and Romanian mafias, have established a foothold in the UAE. These groups are involved in various criminal activities, such as drug trafficking, human trafficking, and organized prostitution, with operations spanning across Europe, the Middle East, and Africa (Lazarević, 2018). Dubai's status as a global transportation and financial hub makes it an ideal base for these criminal organizations to coordinate their transnational criminal enterprises (Lazarević, 2018).

The presence of Russian and Eastern European mafias in the UAE has raised concerns about the city's ability to effectively combat organized crime, particularly in the areas of law enforcement and judicial cooperation. While the UAE has made some efforts to strengthen its legal framework and enhance its law enforcement capacity, critics argue that more needs to be done to ensure that the country's institutions are equipped to deal with the growing threat posed by transnational criminal organizations (Lazarević, 2018).

In order to effectively address the issue of Russian and Eastern European mafias operating in the UAE, the government must adopt a multi-pronged approach that includes enhancing its legal framework, bolstering its law enforcement capacity, fostering international cooperation, and raising public awareness about the dangers posed by organized crime (Lazarević, 2018). Additionally, the UAE should work closely with regional partners and countries of origin for these criminal organizations to share intelligence and coordinate efforts to dismantle criminal networks operating across national borders.

The presence of Russian and Eastern European mafias in the UAE, particularly in Dubai, poses a significant challenge to the city's security and reputation as a safe and attractive destination for international investors and tourists. Addressing this issue will require concerted efforts on the part of the UAE government and its regional and international partners to strengthen legal frameworks, enhance law enforcement capacity, and promote cooperation in the fight against transnational organized crime.

3. Latin American Drug Cartels

Dubai has witnessed the presence of Latin American drug cartels, primarily from Colombia and Mexico. These groups are primarily involved in the trafficking of cocaine and other narcotics into the UAE and use the city as a hub for their global operations (U.S. Department of State, 2020). They also collaborate with local criminals and other international crime syndicates to expand their networks and maintain a steady supply of drugs to the UAE and other countries (Reuter, 2020).

The United Arab Emirates (UAE), particularly Dubai, has increasingly become a hotspot for Latin American drug cartels to invest and launder their illicit proceeds. The city's strategic location, rapid development, and attractive investment opportunities have drawn the attention of powerful drug trafficking organizations from Mexico and other Latin American countries (El Universal, 2019).

Mexican drug cartels, including the Sinaloa Cartel and the Jalisco New Generation Cartel, have been known to invest in Dubai's real estate sector, using the city as a base to launder their drug money (El Universal, 2019). These organizations often rely on local partners and front companies to purchase high-end properties and carry out other financial transactions, thereby obfuscating the true origins of their funds (El Universal, 2019). In addition to real estate, Mexican cartels have also been reported to invest in other sectors, such as luxury goods and hospitality, further expanding their presence in the UAE (El Universal, 2019).

The presence of Latin American drug cartels in the UAE has raised concerns about the city's ability to effectively combat money laundering and maintain its reputation as a safe and attractive destination for international investors and tourists. While the UAE has made efforts to strengthen its anti-money laundering (AML) regulations and improve its financial transparency, critics argue that more needs to be done to ensure that the country's financial system is not exploited by criminal organizations (El Universal, 2019).

In order to address the issue of Latin American drug cartels operating in the UAE, the government must adopt a comprehensive approach that includes enhancing its AML framework, bolstering its law enforcement capacity, fostering international cooperation, and raising public awareness about the dangers posed by organized crime (El Universal, 2019). Additionally, the UAE should work closely with regional partners and countries of origin for these criminal organizations to share intelligence and coordinate efforts to dismantle criminal networks operating across national borders.

Moreover, the UAE should focus on improving the transparency and oversight of its financial sector, particularly in the areas of beneficial ownership and customer due diligence. This would help to ensure that the country's financial institutions are not used as conduits for illicit funds and would make it more difficult for drug cartels to use front companies and complex ownership structures to launder their money (El Universal, 2019). Furthermore, the UAE should continue to invest in training and capacity building for its law enforcement and regulatory agencies, enabling them to better identify, investigate, and prosecute money laundering cases related to Latin American drug cartels and other organized crime groups (El Universal, 2019).

International cooperation and information sharing are also crucial in combating the activities of Latin American drug cartels in the UAE. By working closely with countries affected by these criminal organizations, the UAE can strengthen its ability to track and disrupt the flow of illicit funds and dismantle transnational criminal networks (El Universal, 2019). This may include participating in joint law enforcement operations, sharing financial intelligence, and providing technical assistance to partner countries in their efforts to combat organized crime and money laundering (El Universal, 2019).

Raising public awareness about the dangers posed by drug cartels and organized crime is another important aspect of addressing this issue in the UAE. By educating the public on the risks associated with money laundering and other criminal activities, the government can encourage citizens to be more vigilant and report suspicious activities to the relevant authorities (El Universal, 2019). This will help to create a culture of compliance and deterrence, making it more difficult for criminal organizations to operate in the UAE.

The presence of Latin American drug cartels in the UAE poses significant challenges for the country's efforts to combat money laundering and maintain its reputation as a safe and attractive destination for international investors and tourists. By adopting a comprehensive approach that includes enhancing its AML framework, bolstering law enforcement capacity, fostering international cooperation, and raising public awareness, the UAE can effectively address this issue and ensure the long-term sustainability, stability, and reputation of the country in the global arena.

4.   African Criminal Networks

African criminal networks, particularly from Nigeria and South Africa, have been known to operate in Dubai, engaging in drug trafficking, human trafficking, and financial fraud (Europol, 2017). These groups often exploit the UAE's strategic location and its diverse, transient population to facilitate their criminal activities and recruit members from various nationalities (Davidson, 2008).

The United Arab Emirates (UAE), and Dubai in particular, have emerged as hubs for various criminal networks, including those originating from Africa. These networks exploit the UAE's financial and trade infrastructure to launder money, smuggle goods, and engage in other illicit activities. One of the most prominent examples of this phenomenon is the gold trade, which has become increasingly entwined with criminal networks from Africa (Middle East Research and Information Project [MERIP], 2023).

Gold smuggling has become a lucrative business for African criminal networks, which exploit weak regulation, corruption, and a lack of transparency in the UAE's gold trade to launder money and finance their operations. African gold, which is often sourced from conflict zones or mined using forced labor, is smuggled into the UAE, where it is refined and sold on the international market (MERIP, 2023). This trade not only enables criminal networks to profit from the exploitation of vulnerable communities in Africa but also undermines efforts to combat money laundering and illicit financial flows in the UAE.

The gold trade is just one example of how African criminal networks have infiltrated the UAE. These networks are also involved in a wide range of other criminal activities, including drug trafficking, human trafficking, and arms smuggling (MERIP, 2023). These activities pose significant challenges for the UAE's efforts to combat organized crime and maintain its reputation as a safe and attractive destination for international investors and tourists.

To address the threat posed by African criminal networks, the UAE must take a comprehensive approach that includes strengthening its legal and regulatory frameworks, enhancing law enforcement capacity, fostering international cooperation, and raising public awareness. First, the UAE should enhance its anti-money laundering (AML) and counter-terrorism financing (CTF) frameworks to better detect and disrupt the flow of illicit funds associated with African criminal networks (MERIP, 2023). This may involve strengthening customer due diligence requirements, implementing risk-based supervision, and increasing the transparency of beneficial ownership information.

Second, the UAE should invest in training and capacity building for its law enforcement and regulatory agencies, enabling them to better identify, investigate, and prosecute cases involving African criminal networks (MERIP, 2023). This may include providing specialized training on investigating complex financial crimes as well as investing in advanced technology and equipment to aid in the detection and analysis of illicit financial flows.

Third, the UAE should work closely with African countries and other international partners to combat the activities of African criminal networks. This may involve participating in joint law enforcement operations, sharing financial intelligence, and providing technical assistance to partner countries in their efforts to combat organized crime and money laundering (MERIP, 2023).

Lastly, raising public awareness about the dangers posed by African criminal networks and the illicit activities they engage in is crucial. By educating the public on the risks associated with money laundering, gold smuggling, and other criminal activities, the government can encourage citizens to be more vigilant and report suspicious activities to the relevant authorities (MERIP, 2023).

   5.   Local Criminal Elements

In addition to these international crime groups, Dubai has also seen the involvement of local criminal elements in organized crime. These individuals often act as facilitators, providing logistical support, local knowledge, and connections to the international cartels and mafias operating in the city (Shelley, 2014). They may also engage in various criminal activities, such as drug trafficking, money laundering, and human smuggling, on behalf of their international counterparts (UNODC, 2016).

While the United Arab Emirates (UAE) has gained a reputation as a hub for international criminal organizations, it is important to also acknowledge the presence and activities of local Emirati criminal elements. These local actors engage in various forms of criminal activity, such as money laundering, fraud, drug trafficking, and cybercrime, posing significant challenges to the UAE's efforts to maintain its status as a safe and attractive destination for business and tourism (U.S. Department of State, 2020).

One of the main areas of concern regarding local criminal elements in the UAE is money laundering. Emirati criminals have been known to exploit the country's financial and trade infrastructure to launder proceeds from various forms of illicit activity, including drug trafficking, corruption, and fraud (U.S. Department of State, 2020). The UAE's relatively lax anti-money laundering (AML) and counter-terrorism financing (CTF) regulations, which give local criminals opportunities to take advantage of flaws in the financial system, exacerbate this issue further (U.S. Department of State, 2020).

Another area of concern is the growing prevalence of cybercrime in the UAE. Local criminal elements have increasingly turned to cybercrime as a means of generating income, targeting both domestic and international victims through tactics such as online fraud, identity theft, and hacking (Gulf News, 2021). The UAE's rapid digitization and technological advancements have created new opportunities for local criminals to exploit, posing significant challenges for law enforcement and cybersecurity professionals.

To effectively combat the activities of local Emirati criminal elements, the UAE must take a comprehensive approach that involves strengthening its legal and regulatory frameworks, enhancing law enforcement capacity, and raising public awareness about the dangers of criminal activity. First, the UAE should continue to improve its AML and CTF frameworks to better detect and disrupt local money laundering activities. This may involve implementing risk-based supervision, enhancing customer due diligence requirements, and increasing transparency around beneficial ownership information (U.S. Department of State, 2020).

Second, the UAE should invest in training and capacity building for its law enforcement and regulatory agencies, enabling them to better identify, investigate, and prosecute cases involving local criminal elements. This may include providing specialized training on investigating complex financial crimes and cybercrimes, as well as investing in advanced technology and equipment to aid in the detection and analysis of criminal activities (Gulf News, 2021).

Finally, the UAE should work to raise public awareness about the dangers posed by local criminal elements and the illicit activities they engage in. By educating the public on the risks associated with money laundering, cybercrime, and other criminal activities, the government can encourage citizens to be more vigilant and report suspicious activities to the relevant authorities (Gulf News, 2021).

In conclusion, Dubai's remarkable rise as a global hub has inevitably attracted a diverse array of drug cartels and mafia members from various regions. The city's rapid development, coupled with its strategic location and international connectivity, has inadvertently created opportunities for these criminal networks to expand their operations and exploit the UAE's resources for their illicit activities. This growing presence of organized crime in Dubai poses a significant challenge to the city's long-term stability, security, and reputation as a safe and attractive destination for business and tourism.

To effectively combat this growing threat, it is crucial for Dubai and the UAE as a whole to adopt a comprehensive and multi-pronged approach. One of the key components of this approach should be strengthening law enforcement capabilities. This involves investing in specialized training and capacity building for law enforcement and regulatory agencies, enabling them to better identify, investigate, and prosecute cases involving organized crime. Additionally, providing advanced technology and equipment to aid in the detection and analysis of criminal activities will be essential to disrupting and dismantling these criminal networks (Europol, 2017).

Enhancing international cooperation is another critical aspect of combating organized crime in Dubai. Given the transnational nature of these criminal networks, it is imperative for the UAE to work closely with other countries and international organizations to share intelligence, coordinate law enforcement efforts, and establish joint task forces to target high-profile criminal figures and dismantle their organizations. Strengthening regional and global partnerships will significantly contribute to the disruption of organized crime activities, making it increasingly difficult for these networks to operate in the UAE (Europol, 2017).

Lastly, raising public awareness about the dangers of organized crime is an essential component of this comprehensive approach. By educating the public on the risks associated with drug cartels, mafia organizations, and other criminal activities, the government can encourage citizens to be more vigilant and report suspicious activities to the relevant authorities. Public awareness campaigns, school programs, and community engagement initiatives can play a crucial role in fostering a culture of intolerance towards organized crime, making it more challenging for these networks to thrive in Dubai and the UAE (Europol, 2017).

In summary, Dubai's extraordinary development and global prominence are undeniable. However, the city must confront the darker side that has emerged as a consequence of its rapid growth and internationalization. Addressing the issues of organized crime, which include drug cartels, mafia networks, and other illicit activities, is crucial to ensuring the long-term sustainability, stability, and reputation of Dubai as a leading global city.

To effectively combat organized crime, Dubai needs to strengthen its law enforcement capabilities. Investment in the education and tools required to provide law enforcement agencies with the knowledge and equipment necessary to combat intricate criminal networks can help achieve this (Europol, 2020). Additionally, the establishment of specialized units dedicated to investigating organized crime can help improve the effectiveness of law enforcement efforts in this area (UNODC, 2016).

Enhanced international cooperation is also essential in addressing organized crime, as these networks often operate across borders and exploit vulnerabilities in different jurisdictions. By collaborating with other countries and international organizations, Dubai can share information, intelligence, and best practices to tackle these sophisticated and ever-evolving threats (FATF, 2020). Participating in joint operations and implementing regional initiatives can further strengthen the capacity of law enforcement agencies to combat organized crime effectively (IMF, 2017).

Moreover, increasing public awareness of organized crime and its detrimental impacts on society is vital to mobilizing support for law enforcement efforts and fostering a culture of lawfulness. This can be achieved through public education campaigns, media engagement, and community outreach programs that aim to inform the public about the dangers of organized crime and the importance of reporting suspicious activities to the authorities (Shelley, 2014).

Implementing these measures, however, is not without its challenges. Organized crime networks are highly adaptable and have shown a remarkable ability to evade detection and prosecution (Europol, 2020). Furthermore, the complex nature of these networks and the involvement of corrupt officials in some cases can create significant obstacles to effective law enforcement efforts (Shelley, 2014).

Despite these challenges, the importance of addressing organized crime in Dubai cannot be overstated. The city's continued success as a global hub for business, tourism, and innovation depends on its ability to maintain a safe and stable environment that is free from the destabilizing influence of organized crime. By strengthening law enforcement capabilities, enhancing international cooperation, and increasing public awareness, Dubai can help ensure its long-term sustainability and reputation as a leading global city.

THE RISE OF ORGANIZED CRIME IN THE UAE

A. Historical Context

1. The Oil Boom and Economic Diversification

The United Arab Emirates (UAE) was able to invest in its growth and modernization because of the financial resources made available by the discovery of oil in the 1960s. According to Kumar and Balfour (2016), as the economy of the nation grew, it was able to entice a wide variety of firms and individuals who were looking for chances in the rising economic sectors, such as banking, real estate, and tourism. On the other hand, the UAE's economy expanded so quickly that it presented chances for criminal organizations to penetrate the country and take advantage of the country's newly acquired wealth for their own nefarious purposes (Shelley, 2014).

The UAE has also experienced another form of oil boom, sanctions evasion oil trading. In the article "UAE Earns Big as Iran Sells Oil to China" (Bourse & Bazaar, 2021), the authors discuss how the United Arab Emirates (UAE) has become a critical intermediary in the illegal trade of Iranian oil to China, despite international sanctions on Iran. This situation has not only allowed Iran to continue exporting its oil but has also provided significant financial benefits to the UAE.

As Iran faces international sanctions due to its nuclear program, its oil exports have been severely impacted, leading the country to resort to smuggling oil to bypass the restrictions. According to the article, China has become Iran's primary customer, purchasing large quantities of Iranian oil at discounted prices (Bourse & Bazaar, 2021). The UAE plays a crucial role in facilitating this illicit trade by providing the necessary infrastructure and services to help Iran circumvent sanctions.

The authors point out that the UAE has become a hub for the "petroleum triangle," the trade route that connects Iran, the UAE, and China in the illegal oil trade. Iranian tankers transport the oil to the UAE, where it is transferred to smaller vessels that blend the Iranian crude with other types of oil to mask its origin. The oil is then shipped to China, where it is purchased at a lower price than the global market rate (Bourse & Bazaar, 2021).

The UAE's role in the illegal oil trade has proven to be financially lucrative. The country earns substantial profits from the fees charged for the use of its port facilities, storage tanks, and blending services, as well as from the financial transactions associated with the trade (Bourse & Bazaar, 2021). Furthermore, the UAE has been able to maintain a low profile, as its activities are difficult to detect and prove due to the complex nature of the petroleum triangle and the blending process.

The article also highlights the potential consequences of the UAE's involvement in the illegal oil trade. The country's participation in these activities undermines international efforts to pressure Iran to comply with the terms of the nuclear agreement and runs the risk of attracting international scrutiny and potential penalties (Bourse & Bazaar, 2021).

In conclusion, the UAE has emerged as a significant intermediary in the illegal trade of Iranian oil to China, reaping substantial financial benefits in the process. While this arrangement has allowed Iran to continue exporting its oil and has bolstered the UAE's economy, it also carries potential risks, including undermining international efforts to address Iran's nuclear program and exposing the UAE to potential sanctions.

   2.   Globalization and Interconnectedness

Because of its advantageous location at the crossroads of East and West, the United Arab Emirates (UAE) has become an important commercial and financial center. According to Hutchings and Guala (2017), the growing interconnection of the country's economy with the global economy has made it easier for commodities, people, and capital to travel over the country's borders. This has provided opportunities for criminal networks to start and extend their activities within the United Arab Emirates (UAE). As a direct consequence of this, the United Arab Emirates has developed into a significant hub for the illegal trade of drugs, weapons, and people (UNODC, 2016).

Because of the huge economic growth and globalization that took place over the same time period, the United Arab Emirates (UAE) has emerged in recent decades as a significant player in the international financial arena. This transformation has been made possible as a direct result of the events that took place during those same decades. However, as a direct result of the country's increased interconnectedness and rapid expansion, its exposure to risks associated with money laundering and other illegal activities has increased. These risks include the possibility of being targeted by organized crime. In this light, it is of the utmost importance for the UAE to address the challenges that are presented by the global position it has and implement policies that effectively prevent the laundering of money and other types of financial crimes (Transparency International, 2020). Specifically, it is absolutely necessary for the UAE to address the challenges that are posed by its position in the world.

Because of globalization and increasing connectivity, the United Arab Emirates (UAE) has experienced a growth in the flow of cash and investments, particularly in its main financial hubs such as Dubai and Abu Dhabi. This is especially true in Dubai and Abu Dhabi. According to Transparency International's report from 2020, the nation's advantageous position, advanced infrastructure, and policies that are friendly to investors have attracted businesses and investors from all over the world to the country. This has helped contribute to the expansion and diversification of the nation's economy. However, as a result of this rapid expansion, opportunities have arisen for dishonest individuals and criminals to exploit the financial system of the UAE for the purpose of money laundering and other illegal activities. These opportunities have been made possible as a direct result of this rapid expansion.

B. Economic Factors and Opportunities

The same factors that have contributed to the United Arab Emirates' (UAE) economic growth have also made the nation an attractive place for organized crime, which has led to an increase in the prevalence of organized crime in the UAE. According to Galeotti (2017), the modern infrastructure, ease of doing business, and financial systems that the UAE possesses have provided the instruments necessary for criminal networks to develop and extend their operations within the UAE. This has allowed the criminal networks to flourish and expand their activities within the UAE.

1. Free Trade Zones and Money Laundering

The UAE's numerous free trade zones (FTZs) have been established to promote economic growth and attract foreign investment by offering tax incentives, simplified customs procedures, and minimal bureaucratic oversight (Al Tamimi & Company, 2018). However, these FTZs have also inadvertently created a conducive environment for money laundering and other financial crimes, as criminal networks take advantage of the relaxed regulations and lack of transparency to launder the proceeds of their illicit activities (FATF, 2020).

The United Arab Emirates (UAE) numerous free trade zones (FTZs), have played a significant role in the country's economic growth and diversification efforts. These designated areas offer various incentives to businesses, such as tax exemptions, simplified customs procedures, and 100% foreign ownership, making them attractive hubs for both local and international companies. However, the same characteristics that have made the UAE's FTZs successful have also made them susceptible to money laundering and sanctions evasion, creating challenges for regulators and law enforcement authorities.

UAE's Free Trade Zones

The UAE boasts more than 45 FTZs, including the Jebel Ali Free Zone in Dubai, the Hamriyah Free Zone in Sharjah, and the Khalifa Industrial Zone in Abu Dhabi (UAE Government, 2020). These zones have attracted a diverse range of businesses, from small enterprises to multinational corporations, in sectors such as logistics, manufacturing, and financial services. The economic benefits generated by the FTZs have contributed to the UAE's overall development and its efforts to reduce its dependence on oil revenues.

Money Laundering Risks

Despite their economic benefits, the UAE's FTZs have also become vulnerable to money laundering activities. The lax regulations, ease of company formation, and limited transparency in these zones create opportunities for criminals to exploit the system and launder the proceeds of their illicit activities (FATF, 2020). Shell companies and front organizations can be easily established in the FTZs, allowing criminals to obscure the true ownership and origins of their assets. This lack of transparency makes it difficult for law enforcement and regulators to identify and track suspicious financial transactions, further exacerbating the problem.

Sanctions Evasion

The UAE's FTZs have also been implicated in sanctions evasion schemes, particularly in relation to Iran. Several reports have highlighted instances where Iranian entities have used the UAE's FTZs to circumvent international sanctions and conduct business with global partners (U.S. Department of the Treasury, 2019). This has raised concerns about the UAE's commitment to upholding international sanctions regimes and its ability to effectively monitor and enforce compliance within its FTZs.

However, as of late, Russia and Iran have been using the UAE as a means to sidestep the sanctions that resulted from the Ukraine conflict. In retaliation for Russia's invasion of Ukraine, the United States of America and the European Union have slapped sanctions on Russia. However, wealthy Russians have been able to get around these sanctions by exploiting legal loopholes in the United Arab Emirates (UAE), which are located in the Middle East (The Soufan Center, 2023).

The free-wheeling economic climate that has been fostered by the leaders of the UAE for a substantial length of time, in addition to its growing gold trade, offers an environment that makes it simpler for Russians to evade sanctions. This environment is provided by the United Arab Emirates (UAE). The view held by the leadership of the UAE that Russia continues to play a significant role in the Middle

East area, most notably in Syria, is reflected in the liberal implementation of sanctions against Russia. This perspective is held because the UAE believes that Russia continues to play an important role in Syria. It is one of the reasons why the United States has been reluctant to penalize the United Arab Emirates for evading sanctions on Russia, despite the fact that other countries have undoubtedly seen this selective enforcement (The Soufan Center, 2023). The United Arab Emirates is still an important security and economic partner for the United States. This is one of the reasons why the United States has been reluctant to penalize the United Arab Emirates for evading sanctions on Russia.

Steps to Address the Challenges

The UAE has taken several steps to address the money laundering and sanctions evasion risks associated with its FTZs. These include implementing stricter regulations, increasing transparency, and enhancing the capacity of its financial intelligence unit (UAE Government, 2021). The UAE has also intensified its cooperation with international partners, such as the Financial Action Task Force (FATF) and the United Nations, to strengthen its anti-money laundering (AML) and counter-terrorist financing (CTF) frameworks.

In conclusion, while the UAE's FTZs have been instrumental in driving the country's economic growth and diversification, they have also presented challenges in the form of money laundering and sanctions evasion. Addressing these issues is essential to safeguarding the integrity of the UAE's financial system and ensuring the continued success of its FTZs as engines of economic development.

2. Real Estate and Construction Boom

Due to the UAE's efforts to diversify its economy and an influx of foreign investment, the real estate and construction sectors have seen rapid growth in recent years. The construction of luxurious residential and commercial properties has attracted high-net-worth individuals and corporations from around the world (Kumar & Balfour, 2016). Unfortunately, this boom has also provided criminal networks with an opportunity to launder their illicit proceeds through the purchase of high-value real estate assets (FATF, 2020).

The author of the piece titled "Dubai: UAE used by foreigners to launder billions through real estate" (Middle East Eye, 2021) notes the rising concern about the role of the United Arab Emirates (UAE), and more specifically Dubai, as a center for money laundering operations involving foreign citizens. According to the report, billions of dollars are being cleaned through the real estate industry in the UAE, which has caused worry among international watchdogs and led to requests for more stringent anti-money laundering measures.

The author cites a report by the Carnegie Endowment for International Peace, which states that the United Arab Emirates (UAE) has attracted individuals and entities from countries such as Russia, Iran, and Afghanistan who are seeking to launder their ill-gotten gains through Dubai's booming real estate market (Middle East Eye, 2021). The report states that these individuals and entities are attracted to the UAE because of Dubai's booming real estate market (Middle East Eye, 2021). According to the research, Dubai's permissive rules, robust property market, and strategic position make it an excellent venue for engaging in operations related to the laundering of illicit funds. In addition, the emirate's free zones and the widespread usage of anonymous shell firms make it possible for criminals to conceal the origins of their finances and avoid identification by the relevant authorities.

In addition to this, the piece highlights the impact that these illegal operations have had on Dubai's reputation as a central location for international commerce. Because of the flow of illegal cash into the real estate industry, property prices have increased, which may discourage genuine investors and businesses from entering the market (Middle East Eye, 2021).

The United Arab Emirates' (UAE's) participation in activities that include money laundering might damage the country's reputation on the world stage and draw the attention of global authorities, which could lead to sanctions or other types of punitive actions.

The United Arab Emirates (UAE) has in recent years adopted a number of new anti-money-laundering rules in order to address these issues. In order to combat issues related to the laundering of funds and the funding of terrorist organizations, the nation has developed a financial intelligence unit and increased its interaction with foreign partners (Middle East Eye, 2021).

The report does highlight, however, that these attempts have been regarded with suspicion by certain experts. These experts claim that the restrictions imposed by the UAE are insufficient to limit the flow of illegal funds via its real estate market. The United Arab Emirates, and Dubai in particular, has emerged as a hotspot for money laundering operations, with foreign nationals leveraging the country's real estate market to launder billions of dollars.

In conclusion, the UAE has become a hotspot for money laundering activities. This issue puts the United Arab Emirates' status as a global commercial powerhouse in jeopardy and may result in the UAE being scrutinized internationally and subjected to potential penalties. Even though the United Arab Emirates (UAE) has recently implemented new anti-money laundering measures, there are still concerns regarding the efficacy of these efforts in addressing the problem.

C. Political and Social Factors

The UAE's political and social landscape has significantly contributed to the growth of organized crime within the nation. Several factors, including corruption, weak governance, and the presence of a diverse and transient population, have created an environment conducive to the expansion and proliferation of criminal networks (Shelley, 2014).

Corruption is one of the primary factors facilitating the growth of organized crime in the UAE. Despite efforts to combat corruption, the country still faces challenges in this area. Graft, bribery, and the abuse of power by officials have allowed criminal networks to operate with relative impunity, undermining the rule of law and creating a climate of distrust in public institutions (Transparency International, 2021). Moreover, the presence of corruption can also deter foreign investment and hinder economic growth, perpetuating a cycle of inequality and social unrest that criminal networks can exploit to their advantage (World Bank, 2016).

Weak governance is another factor that has contributed to the rise of organized crime in the UAE. The country's rapid development has, in some cases, outpaced the ability of its regulatory and law enforcement agencies to effectively monitor and control criminal activities. The government has found it challenging to address the growing threat that organized crime poses due to a lack of oversight, inadequate legal systems, and insufficient funding (Carnegie Endowment for International Peace, 2020). This, in turn, has allowed criminal networks to operate with relative freedom, further exacerbating the issue.

The UAE's diverse and transient population has also played a role in fostering an environment in which organized crime can thrive. As a major international hub, the UAE attracts a large number of foreign workers and expatriates, many of whom are seeking temporary employment or residency. This constant influx of people creates opportunities for criminal networks to exploit vulnerable individuals, recruit new members, and establish connections with other criminal organizations across the globe (Koser, 2016). The transient nature of the population also makes it more challenging for law enforcement agencies to track and monitor criminal activities, as individuals may quickly enter and exit the country with limited scrutiny (Shelley, 2014).

The UAE's political and social landscape has played a critical role in enabling the growth of organized crime within the nation. To effectively combat this issue, the UAE must address the root causes that have allowed criminal networks to flourish. This involves tackling corruption, strengthening governance structures, and addressing the challenges posed by the country's diverse and transient population. By adopting a comprehensive and targeted approach, the UAE can work towards creating a safer and more secure environment for its citizens and residents.

1. Corruption and Weak Governance

While the UAE has made significant progress in addressing corruption and improving governance in recent years, challenges remain. Corruption within the public sector, particularly in areas such as customs, immigration, and law enforcement, can enable criminal networks to operate with relative impunity (Transparency International, 2019). Furthermore, the complex and often opaque regulatory environment in the UAE can create opportunities for criminals to exploit loopholes and circumvent anti-money laundering (AML) and counter-terrorism financing (CTF) measures (FATF, 2020).

The writers of the piece titled "South Africa's Gupta Brothers Are Back — in Dubai" (which appeared in The New York Times in 2023) explore the case of the Gupta brothers, who have been accused of corruption in South Africa, as well as their present activities in the United Arab Emirates (UAE), notably in Dubai. The piece is titled "South Africa's Gupta Brothers Are Back — in Dubai." This case draws attention to the role that Dubai plays as a sanctuary for persons and organizations involved in illegal activities and raises issues about the commitment of the United Arab Emirates to tackling corruption and money laundering.

According to The New York Times (2023), the Gupta brothers, Atul, Ajay, and Rajesh, are businessmen who were born in India and have been linked to a number of corruption scandals in South Africa. These scandals involve their close association with a previous president of South Africa named Jacob Zuma. The brothers are accused of leveraging their political connections to get lucrative government contracts, engaging in bribery, and laundering money through offshore firms in order to enrich themselves financially. By moving to Dubai, the Gupta brothers have been able to avoid being brought to justice, despite the fact that they are wanted for several crimes in South Africa and are the subject of an international arrest warrant.

According to the piece, which was published in The New York Times in 2023, Dubai has become a safe haven for the Gupta brothers, allowing them to continue running their businesses there while still preserving their lavish lifestyle. The writers make note of the fact that the United Arab Emirates (UAE) has not taken any serious action against the Guptas despite the fact that South African authorities have requested their extradition on many occasions. Because of this lack of collaboration, concerns have been raised concerning the role that Dubai plays in supporting corruption and money laundering, as well as the efficiency of the steps that Dubai takes to combat money laundering.

The writers contend that the UAE's unwillingness to take action against the Gupta brothers is symptomatic of a larger problem since the nation has become a center for persons and organizations engaging in unlawful operations (The New York Times, 2023). They make this argument in a piece that was published in The New York Times. The Financial Action Task Force (FATF) listed the United Arab Emirates as a high-risk jurisdiction for money laundering and terrorism financing in a study that was cited in the article. According to the report, the UAE is a high-risk jurisdiction because of its inadequate legislation, weak enforcement, and abundance of anonymous shell firms. The research also mentioned that the United Arab Emirates' free trade zones and real estate industry are particularly susceptible to misuse by criminals who are attempting to escape sanctions and wash money through illicit means.

The author of the piece, which was published in The New York Times in 2023, draws attention to the fact that the conclusion of the piece is that if the United Arab Emirates (UAE) does not solve these challenges, it might have severe repercussions for both its worldwide reputation and its ties with important allies. The writers make note of the fact that the United Arab Emirates (UAE) has been the target of criticism from both the European Union and the United States for its involvement in supporting corruption and money laundering. This criticism has the potential to result in sanctions or other forms of punitive action. The scandal involving the Gupta brothers serves as a sobering reminder of the difficulties that the UAE must overcome if it is to be successful in its efforts to address the problem of organized crime and illegal money flows.

   2.   A Diverse and Transient Population

The UAE's rapid economic growth and global reputation as a desirable destination for expatriates have attracted a diverse and transient population from around the world (Kumar & Balfour, 2016). While the majority of these individuals are law-abiding residents seeking a better quality of life and economic opportunities, this diverse population also includes individuals with criminal backgrounds and connections to organized crime (Shelley, 2014). This situation can make it difficult for law enforcement agencies to identify and track criminal networks operating within the UAE.

However, transient populations can create problems. The author of "Israeli Criminals Flee to Dubai to Escape Arrest" (The New Arab, 2020) tackles the topic of Israeli criminals seeking sanctuary in Dubai, taking advantage of the city's loose investment regulations and its strategic position. The article is titled "Israeli Criminals Flee to Dubai to Escape Arrest." The article focuses on the difficulties that Dubai is experiencing in its fight against organized crime and the ramifications that this situation has on the reputation of the UAE in the international community.

According to the author of "The New Arab, 2020," in recent years, scores of Israeli criminals have fled to Dubai in order to avoid prosecution in Israel and other countries and have found refuge there. These people are involved in a variety of illegal endeavors, such as the distribution of illegal drugs, the laundering of illicit funds, and the operation of an organized criminal enterprise. The report says that these criminals are drawn to Dubai owing to its strategic location as a worldwide center, as well as its investment-friendly atmosphere and comparatively weak law enforcement. These factors combine to make Dubai an attractive destination for crooks. Additionally, the recent normalization of relations between Israel and the UAE has made it easier for Israeli nationals to move to the nation that is located in the Gulf.

According to the information presented in the article (The New Arab, 2020), Israeli criminals in Dubai are engaged in a variety of illegal operations, including the formation of shell businesses, the laundering of money, and the distribution of illegal drugs. The author provides an illustration of an Israeli drug kingpin who was only recently apprehended in Dubai after escaping detection for a number of years in other countries. The case highlights the difficulties that Dubai's law enforcement authorities confront in combating organized crime and the complicated networks that allow criminals to operate with relative impunity. These difficulties were brought to light by the recent case.

The author also emphasizes the possible repercussions that this behavior may have for Dubai's worldwide reputation and its relationships with important partners (The New Arab, 2020). The fact that criminals from Israel are present in the city calls into question the efficiency of the United Arab Emirates' efforts to combat money laundering and the funding of terrorism, as well as its dedication to the fight against organized crime. According to the information presented in the article, the United Arab Emirates (UAE) might suffer harm to its credibility and face heightened scrutiny from international organizations such as the Financial Action Task Force (FATF) if it does not address this issue.

The piece highlights how important it is for Dubai to take immediate action against Israeli criminals and other elements of organized crime that are working within its boundaries (The New Arab, 2020). This involves increasing the capacities of law enforcement agencies, enhancing coordination with foreign partners, and putting into place more stringent measures to combat money laundering and the funding of terrorist organizations. The United Arab Emirates (UAE) can strengthen its efforts to combat organized crime and illegal financial flows and safeguard its status as a worldwide hub for commerce, finance, and investment if it takes these concerns seriously and finds solutions to them.

D. The Emergence of Drug Cartels and Mafia in the UAE

The confluence of economic, political, and social factors outlined above has led to the establishment and growth of drug cartels and mafia organizations within the UAE. These criminal networks have capitalized on the opportunities presented by the nation's economic success and global interconnectedness to expand their operations and forge alliances with local and international criminal groups (Galeotti, 2017).

In the article "Dubai's Role in Facilitating Corruption and Global Illicit Financial Flows" (Carnegie Endowment for International Peace, 2020), the author examines the growing concerns surrounding the United Arab Emirates (UAE) and its role in enabling corruption and illicit financial flows worldwide. The article focuses on Dubai, which has emerged as a key hub for money laundering and other criminal activities due to its strategic location, business-friendly environment, and lax regulations.

The author highlights that Dubai's real estate sector has been particularly susceptible to illicit financial activities, as it attracts a large amount of foreign investment and offers a high degree of anonymity to buyers (Carnegie Endowment, 2020). The article cites a report by the Carnegie Endowment for International Peace, which found that Dubai's property market has been used to launder money from countries such as Russia, Iran, and Afghanistan. The report also revealed that several high-profile individuals and organizations involved in corruption and other illicit activities have used Dubai's real estate sector to hide their assets and evade international sanctions.

In addition to the real estate sector, the article points out that Dubai's free trade zones and its extensive network of offshore companies have also facilitated money laundering and other criminal activities (Carnegie Endowment, 2020). The free trade zones offer significant tax and regulatory advantages to businesses, which can be exploited by criminals to launder money and evade detection by authorities. Moreover, the widespread use of anonymous shell companies allows individuals and entities to obscure the origin of their funds and avoid scrutiny from regulators.

Many argue that Dubai's role in facilitating corruption and illicit financial flows poses significant risks to the UAE's international reputation and its relationships with key partners (Carnegie Endowment, 2020). The author notes that the UAE has faced criticism from organizations such as the Financial Action Task Force

(FATF) and the European Union for its lack of effective anti-money laundering measures and its vulnerability to financial crime. This criticism could potentially lead to sanctions or other punitive measures, which would negatively impact the UAE's economy and global standing.

To address these concerns, the UAE has taken steps to strengthen its anti-money laundering framework and enhance its cooperation with international partners (Carnegie Endowment, 2020). However, the article suggests that these measures may not be sufficient to fully address the problem, as the UAE continues to face challenges in enforcing its regulations and combating the flow of illicit funds through its financial system.

The UAE, particularly Dubai, has emerged as a significant facilitator of corruption and illicit financial flows worldwide. The country's real estate sector, free trade zones, and the prevalence of anonymous shell companies have enabled money laundering and other criminal activities. Despite recent efforts to strengthen its anti-money laundering framework, concerns remain about the UAE's ability to effectively combat the issue.

1. Drug Cartels

Drug cartels have increasingly targeted the UAE as a key transit point for the trafficking of narcotics between producer countries, such as Afghanistan, and consumer markets in Europe, Asia, and Africa (UNODC, 2016). The UAE's advanced infrastructure, strategic location, and ease of doing business have made it an attractive hub for drug traffickers seeking to smuggle narcotics through the country enroute to other destinations (Hutchings & Guala, 2017).

The UAE's well-developed transportation networks, including its state-of-the-art seaports and airports, have facilitated the movement of illicit goods by drug cartels. These infrastructures provide multiple entry and exit points, making it challenging for law enforcement agencies to monitor and intercept drug shipments effectively (Reitano & Clarke, 2016). Furthermore, the UAE's status as a regional trade hub has led to a significant volume of goods passing through its borders daily, enabling drug traffickers to hide illicit substances within legitimate cargo shipments, further complicating detection efforts (Koser, 2016).

The UAE's strategic location at the crossroads of major global trade routes has also made it an attractive destination for drug cartels. Positioned between Asia, Europe, and Africa, the UAE serves as a crucial transit point for narcotics moving between these regions (Reitano & Clarke, 2016). This geographic advantage enables drug traffickers to take advantage of established trade routes and exploit the country's role as a regional economic powerhouse (Hutchings & Guala, 2017).

Additionally, the ease of doing business in the UAE has attracted legitimate entrepreneurs and investors, but it has also inadvertently created opportunities for criminal networks. The country's pro-business environment, including its favorable tax policies and minimal bureaucratic red tape, has made it easier for drug cartels to establish front companies and launder proceeds from their illicit activities (U.S. Department of State, 2020). Moreover, the UAE's complex corporate structures and financial secrecy laws can make it difficult for law enforcement agencies to trace and dismantle these criminal enterprises (Transparency International, 2021).

The UAE has put in place a number of measures to combat drug trafficking, such as improving its law enforcement capabilities, bolstering border security, and encouraging international cooperation (U.S. Department of State, 2020). However, the continued presence of drug cartels in the UAE underscores the need for a more comprehensive and coordinated approach to address this issue effectively.

2. Mafia Organizations

Due to the wealth and opportunities for money laundering, financial crimes, and other illegal activities in the UAE, mafia groups have also established a presence there. These organizations have infiltrated various sectors of the UAE's economy, including real estate, construction, and financial services, using their criminal proceeds to fund their operations and expand their influence (Galeotti, 2017).

Mafia organizations operating in the UAE are often transnational, with links to criminal networks in other countries, particularly Russia, Eastern Europe, Italy, and Latin America (Europol, 2017). The international nature of these groups enables them to leverage their global connections and expertise to expand their illicit activities within the UAE and beyond (Shelley, 2014).

One of the primary reasons mafia organizations are attracted to the UAE is the country's well-developed financial infrastructure and its status as a global financial center. The UAE's banking system, offshore financial centers, and free trade zones provide ample opportunities for money laundering and other financial crimes, making it an attractive destination for criminal groups seeking to hide and launder their illicit proceeds (FATF, 2020). In addition, the UAE's strict bank secrecy laws and complex corporate structures make it difficult for law enforcement agencies to trace and seize criminal assets, further incentivizing mafia groups to operate within the country (Transparency International, 2021).

Mafia organizations have also targeted the real estate and construction industries in the UAE because they offer numerous opportunities for corruption and money laundering. Criminal groups often invest their illicit proceeds in high-value properties, which can be used to legitimize their wealth and facilitate further criminal activities (OCCRP, 2020). In addition, the construction industry in the UAE is characterized by complex contracting arrangements and a lack of transparency, making it vulnerable to infiltration by organized crime groups (Transparency International, 2021).

To summarize, a combination of historical, economic, political, and social factors is to blame for the rise of organized crime in the UAE. As the nation continues its impressive journey of growth and development, it must also confront the challenges posed by the presence of drug cartels and mafia organizations within its borders. By understanding the complex dynamics of organized crime in the UAE, policymakers and law enforcement agencies can develop targeted and effective strategies to combat this growing menace and ensure the continued success and prosperity of the nation.

Due to its enormous oil wealth, the UAE has historically experienced rapid economic development, which has resulted in significant social and demographic changes. The influx of foreign workers and the diversification of the economy have created opportunities for criminal networks to establish a foothold in the country (Koser, 2016). The multicultural and transient nature of the UAE's population has also made it more challenging for law enforcement agencies to monitor and control the activities of organized crime groups (Europol, 2017).

Economically, the UAE's status as a global financial center, trade hub, and regional powerhouse has made it an attractive destination for drug cartels and mafia organizations seeking to expand their operations and launder their illicit proceeds (FATF, 2020). The country's well-developed infrastructure and ease of doing business have also facilitated the growth of organized crime by enabling criminal networks to move goods, people, and money across borders with relative ease (Reitano & Clarke, 2016).

Politically, the UAE's governance structures have, at times, struggled to keep pace with the rapid growth and diversification of the economy, leading to weaknesses in law enforcement, regulatory oversight, and anti-corruption efforts (Transparency International, 2021). Organized crime groups have taken advantage of these flaws by infiltrating different economic sectors and establishing networks of influence and corruption (Shelley, 2014).

Inequality, social unrest, and a lack of knowledge about the dangers posed by drug cartels and mafia organizations are just a few social factors that have made organized crime in the UAE worse. The disparity between the wealthy and the poor has created an environment in which criminal networks can recruit members and exploit vulnerable individuals for their illicit activities (Borgen Project, 2021). Furthermore, a lack of public awareness about the extent and impact of organized crime in the UAE has hampered efforts to mobilize public support for measures to combat this threat (Europol, 2017).

In conclusion, a range of historical, economic, political, and social factors have contributed to the rise of organized crime in the UAE. To address these challenges effectively, the country must continue to invest in law enforcement and regulatory capacity, strengthen its anti-corruption and anti-money laundering frameworks, and raise public awareness about the dangers posed by drug cartels and mafia organizations. By tackling organized crime head-on, the UAE can safeguard its continued growth, development, and prosperity for future generations.

THE DRUG TRADE IN THE UAE

A. Narcotics Distribution Networks

    1.   Overview

Drug trafficking networks have established a significant presence in the United Arab Emirates (UAE), primarily using the nation as a transit point for narcotics enroute to other destinations (UNODC, 2016). The UAE's strategic location, advanced infrastructure, and global connectivity make it an attractive hub for these networks, which exploit these attributes to move large quantities of drugs, primarily heroin and synthetic drugs, from producer countries to consumer markets in Europe, Asia, and Africa (Hutchings & Guala, 2017).

Key drug trafficking routes include the so-called 'Balkan route' and the 'Southern route,' which connect opium-producing regions in Afghanistan and Pakistan to consumer markets in Europe and beyond (UNODC, 2016). These routes have facilitated the smuggling of significant quantities of heroin through the UAE, with traffickers using various methods to conceal their illicit cargoes, such as hiding drugs in legitimate cargo shipments or using drug mules to transport narcotics through international airports (Hutchings & Guala, 2017).

The illicit drug trade has also been linked to other forms of organized crime in the UAE, including money laundering, human trafficking, and arms trafficking (UNODC, 2016). These criminal activities often intersect, with drug traffickers relying on other criminal networks to launder their proceeds, transport drugs, and provide logistical support (Hutchings & Guala, 2017).

Synthetic drugs, such as methamphetamine and synthetic cannabinoids, have also emerged as a significant challenge for the UAE. These substances, often produced in clandestine laboratories in Asia or Europe, are smuggled into the country, where they are distributed to local markets or re-exported to other countries in the region (UNODC, 2016).

2. Transportation Methods

Drug traffickers employ a variety of methods to move narcotics through the UAE, capitalizing on the country's advanced transportation infrastructure and global connectivity. Some of the most common methods include:

a. Air Cargo: Traffickers often conceal narcotics within legitimate cargo shipments or courier parcels that transit through the UAE's busy airports, such as Dubai International Airport and Abu Dhabi International Airport (UNODC, 2016). The sheer volume of cargo traffic makes it difficult for law enforcement to detect and intercept illicit drug shipments, especially when they are skillfully hidden within legal goods. In some cases, drug mules are also used to transport narcotics through international airports, carrying drugs on their person or in their luggage (Hutchings & Guala, 2017).

b. Maritime Shipping: Traffickers exploit the UAE's extensive coastline and numerous ports to smuggle drugs on board commercial vessels, fishing boats, and pleasure craft (Hutchings & Guala, 2017). The country's location along major shipping routes and its role as a global hub for maritime trade make it an attractive target for drug traffickers seeking to move large quantities of narcotics by sea. In some instances, traffickers use "mother ships" to transport drugs to smaller vessels off the coast, which then deliver the narcotics to shore or other waiting ships.

c. Overland Routes: Traffickers also use land routes to move drugs through the UAE, either by road in private vehicles or hidden among legitimate goods transported by trucks (UNODC, 2016). The UAE's extensive road network and its connections to neighboring countries facilitate the movement of drugs across borders and into the country. Traffickers often use well-established smuggling routes and employ various tactics, such as the use of "decoy" vehicles, to evade detection by law enforcement.

To effectively combat drug trafficking in the UAE, it is crucial for law enforcement agencies to continuously adapt and develop innovative strategies to detect and disrupt these transportation methods. This requires a multifaceted approach that includes intelligence gathering, inter-agency cooperation, and the use of advanced technology, such as x-ray scanners and K-9 units, to identify and intercept drug shipments. Furthermore, enhancing cooperation and information sharing with regional and international partners is essential to dismantling the transnational criminal networks that drive the drug trade and exploit the UAE's transportation infrastructure for their illicit activities.

3.   Distribution Channels

Once narcotics enter the UAE, they are typically stored in safe houses or warehouses before being re-exported to other destinations. Traffickers often use complex distribution channels and employ local intermediaries to facilitate the onward movement of drugs, which may involve multiple handovers and transportation methods to avoid detection by law enforcement authorities (UNODC, 2016).

These safe houses and warehouses are usually located in discreet areas or hidden among legitimate businesses to minimize the risk of discovery by law enforcement. In some cases, drugs are repackaged or modified to further conceal their true nature and make them more difficult to detect during subsequent transportation (UNODC, 2016).

Local intermediaries play a crucial role in the drug trade, acting as brokers and facilitators between traffickers and their clients. These individuals may be involved in various stages of the drug supply chain, such as arranging transportation, managing storage facilities, and coordinating the distribution of narcotics to buyers. Intermediaries typically have a deep understanding of the local environment and possess the necessary contacts and resources to ensure the smooth flow of drugs through the UAE (UNODC, 2016).

The complex distribution channels employed by traffickers are designed to create multiple layers of separation between the drugs and their ultimate destination, making it more challenging for law enforcement to track and intercept shipments. This may involve using different transportation methods, such as switching from air to land or sea transport or routing drugs through multiple countries to obfuscate their true origin and destination (UNODC, 2016).

Furthermore, traffickers often use advanced technology and encryption tools to communicate and coordinate their activities, making it difficult for law enforcement agencies to intercept and decode their communications. This highlights the need for enhanced technical capabilities and specialized training for law enforcement personnel to stay ahead of the evolving tactics employed by drug traffickers (UNODC, 2016).

In order to disrupt and dismantle the complex distribution networks used by drug traffickers in the UAE, it is crucial for law enforcement agencies to adopt a proactive and intelligence-led approach. This involves the gathering and analysis of information to identify patterns and trends, which can then be used to target key nodes within the drug supply chain. Additionally, fostering greater collaboration and information sharing between national and international law enforcement partners is essential to effectively combating the transnational nature of drug trafficking and strengthening the global response to this pervasive threat.

B. The Role of Local and International Players

1.   Local Criminal Networks

Local criminal networks play a crucial role in the drug trade within the UAE, providing logistical support and local knowledge to international trafficking organizations. These local networks are often composed of UAE nationals and foreign residents with ties to organized crime groups in their home countries (Shelley, 2014). They may act as facilitators, brokers, or transporters, helping to move drugs through the UAE and liaising with international trafficking organizations (UNODC, 2016).

These local criminal networks typically operate in close-knit groups, often bound by familial or ethnic ties, which can make it difficult for law enforcement agencies to infiltrate and dismantle their operations (Shelley, 2014). The close relationships between members of these networks also foster a sense of loyalty and trust, making it less likely for individuals to cooperate with authorities or divulge information about their criminal activities (UNODC, 2016).

In addition to facilitating drug trafficking, local criminal networks in the UAE may also engage in other illicit activities, such as money laundering, corruption, and the smuggling of contraband goods. These activities generate significant profits for the networks, which can be reinvested into their drug trafficking operations or used to fund other criminal endeavors (Shelley, 2014).

The involvement of local criminal networks in the drug trade presents significant challenges for law enforcement agencies in the UAE. These networks are often highly adaptable and resilient, capable of quickly adjusting their tactics and methods in response to law enforcement pressure (UNODC, 2016). Moreover, their close connections to international trafficking organizations enable them to access a wide range of resources and expertise, further complicating efforts to combat their activities.

To effectively address the threat posed by local criminal networks, law enforcement agencies in the UAE must develop targeted strategies that focus on disrupting the key nodes within these networks, such as the facilitators, brokers, and transporters. This can be achieved through the use of intelligence-led policing, which involves the collection, analysis, and dissemination of information to inform operational decision-making (UNODC, 2016).

Furthermore, enhancing cooperation and information sharing between local, regional, and international law enforcement partners is essential to combating the transnational nature of these networks. By working together and leveraging their respective resources and expertise, law enforcement agencies can develop a more comprehensive understanding of the complex dynamics of local criminal networks and devise more effective strategies to disrupt their activities and dismantle their operations.

2. International Trafficking Organizations

The United Arab Emirates (UAE) has emerged as a significant transit point for international drug trafficking organizations, thanks to its strategic location and extensive global connectivity. A number of these organizations have managed to establish a strong presence in the country, taking advantage of its booming economy and world-class infrastructure. In this article, we delve into the activities of four major international drug trafficking networks operating in the UAE: Afghan, Iranian, South Asian, and Nigerian.

a. Afghan Networks: Afghanistan, being the world's largest producer of opium and heroin, has seen its trafficking networks make significant inroads in the UAE (UNODC, 2016). These networks often maintain links to the Taliban and other insurgent groups, relying on the drug trade's lucrative revenues to finance their activities (Shelley, 2014). The UAE's proximity to Afghanistan and its excellent transportation infrastructure have made it an attractive hub for these networks. They use various means to smuggle narcotics, such as hiding drugs in legal cargo shipments or employing human couriers, often known as "mules," who ingest drug-filled capsules or conceal them in their luggage.

b. Iranian Networks: Iranian trafficking networks have also established a presence in the UAE, taking advantage of the close proximity between the two countries and their shared maritime borders (Hutchings & Guala, 2017). Iran's lengthy coastline along the Persian Gulf and the Gulf of Oman provides ample opportunities for drug traffickers to use maritime routes to smuggle narcotics. The use of high-speed boats, fishing vessels, and commercial shipping containers enables them to move drugs through the region with relative ease. Once inside the UAE, these drugs are then distributed to various countries around the world, including Europe, Asia, and Africa.

c. South Asian Networks: Drug traffickers from South Asian countries, such as Pakistan and India, have also found the UAE to be an attractive location for their operations (UNODC, 2016). They are primarily focused on the trafficking of heroin and synthetic drugs, such as methamphetamine and various "designer drugs." South Asian networks often rely on the UAE's extensive air and sea connections to move their narcotics consignments, using similar methods to those employed by Afghan and Iranian networks. In addition, they have been known to leverage the large South Asian expatriate community in the UAE to facilitate their activities, making it easier to blend in and evade detection.

d. Nigerian Networks: In recent years, Nigerian trafficking organizations have increasingly targeted the UAE as a key transit point for cocaine shipments originating from South America and destined for Europe and Asia (Hutchings & Guala, 2017). Nigeria is strategically located along the West African coast, making it an ideal staging point for drug shipments across the Atlantic. The UAE's central location between Europe, Africa, and Asia, coupled with its excellent infrastructure, has made it an attractive destination for Nigerian traffickers looking to move their illicit goods onward.

These Nigerian networks often use human couriers, or "mules," to transport drugs, as well as exploit commercial air and sea routes to move large quantities of narcotics. They have also been known to collaborate with local criminal organizations in the UAE to facilitate their operations, further entrenching their presence in the country.

In conclusion, the UAE's strategic location and extensive global connectivity have made it an attractive hub for international drug trafficking organizations. The presence of Afghan, Iranian, South Asian, and Nigerian networks in the country poses significant challenges to law enforcement and the wider society, as the drug trade often fuels other criminal activities and undermines the rule of law. To combat these networks, the UAE government has been working closely with international partners, such as the United Nations Office on Drugs and Crime (UNODC), to enhance its counter-narcotics capabilities and develop comprehensive strategies to dismantle them.

C. The Impact on the UAE Society and Economy

    1. Social Impact

The drug trade in the UAE, fueled by the presence of international drug trafficking organizations, has had several negative consequences for the nation's society. Among these consequences are the growth of drug addiction, particularly among young people, and an increase in crime and violence. In this article, we discuss the implications of these consequences in further detail:

a. Drug Addiction: Although the UAE is primarily a transit country for drug trafficking, drug addiction has become a growing problem within the nation, especially among young people (Alhyas, Elarabi, & AlGhaferi, 2015). The easy availability of narcotics in the UAE has resulted in an increase in substance abuse and addiction, with a particularly high prevalence of heroin and synthetic drug use (WHO, 2019). This has placed a significant burden on the country's healthcare system as well as on families and communities affected by addiction.

The rising rates of drug addiction have prompted the UAE government to invest in prevention and treatment programs. These efforts include launching public awareness campaigns to educate the population about the dangers of drug use as well as establishing rehabilitation centers that provide comprehensive care and support for individuals struggling with addiction. Moreover, the government has tightened its drug control policies, imposing strict penalties for drug possession and trafficking in an effort to deter potential users and traffickers.

b. Crime and Violence: The drug trade has also contributed to an increase in crime and violence in the UAE, as criminal networks engage in turf wars, extortion, and other forms of criminal activity to protect their interests (Shelley, 2014). These activities not only jeopardize public safety but also undermine the rule of law, particularly in areas with a strong presence of drug trafficking organizations. The UAE has long been known for its low crime rates and overall safety; however, the presence of international drug trafficking networks threatens to erode this reputation.

The rise in drug-related crime and violence has led to an increased demand for law enforcement resources as police and other security forces work to dismantle criminal organizations and disrupt their operations. This has prompted the UAE government to invest in training and equipping its law enforcement agencies with the necessary tools to combat the drug trade effectively. Moreover, the government has sought to strengthen its cooperation with international partners, such as the United Nations Office on Drugs and Crime (UNODC), to enhance its counter-narcotics capabilities and develop comprehensive strategies to tackle the issue.

In addition to the direct consequences of drug addiction and crime, the drug trade has also had negative effects on the UAE's economy. The illicit drug trade generates enormous profits, but these funds are often laundered through legitimate businesses or channeled into other criminal activities, undermining the integrity of the nation's financial system. In order to reduce the risk that drug-related financial crimes pose, the UAE has implemented stringent anti-money laundering and counter-terrorist financing regulations.

Furthermore, the presence of drug trafficking organizations can lead to a loss of investor confidence, as some may be deterred from investing in a country perceived to have a significant drug problem. This can hinder the nation's economic growth and development in the long run. Therefore, the UAE's efforts to combat the drug trade are crucial not only for ensuring public safety and health but also for maintaining its economic stability and global reputation.

2. Economic Impact

The drug trade in the UAE has far-reaching economic implications that extend beyond the direct consequences of drug addiction and crime. Two significant issues arising from the drug trade are money laundering and corruption, both of which can have severe consequences for the UAE's economy and reputation. In this article, we discuss these issues in more detail, as well as the measures the UAE has taken to address them.

a. Money Laundering: The proceeds of drug trafficking are often laundered through the UAE's financial system, real estate market, and other sectors of the economy (FATF, 2020). Money laundering activities can undermine the integrity of the UAE's financial system, exposing the nation to reputational risks and potential sanctions from international organizations such as the International Monetary Fund (IMF, 2017). The UAE's role as an international financial center and its well-developed real estate market makes it particularly vulnerable to money laundering risks associated with the drug trade.

To combat money laundering, the UAE has implemented strict anti-money laundering (AML) and counter-terrorist financing (CTF) regulations, which require financial institutions to maintain robust compliance programs and report suspicious transactions to the authorities. The UAE has also established a Financial Intelligence Unit (FIU) to analyze and disseminate financial intelligence related to money laundering and terrorist financing activities. Furthermore, the UAE actively participates in international AML/CTF initiatives and engages with international partners to enhance its capacity to combat money laundering.

b. Corruption: The drug trade can also contribute to corruption within the UAE, as criminal networks seek to infiltrate and co-opt public officials, law enforcement agencies, and other institutions to facilitate their activities (Transparency International, 2019). The involvement of public officials in the drug trade can weaken governance, undermine the effectiveness of anti-corruption efforts, and erode public trust in the UAE's institutions.

In response to the corruption risks posed by the drug trade, the UAE has taken significant steps to strengthen its anti-corruption framework. These measures include the establishment of dedicated anti-corruption agencies, the enactment of comprehensive anti-corruption legislation, and the promotion of transparency and accountability in public administration. The UAE is also a signatory to the United Nations Convention Against Corruption (UNCAC), which demonstrates its commitment to international anti-corruption standards and best practices.

Moreover, the UAE has sought to enhance the capacity of its law enforcement agencies to detect and investigate corruption cases, including those linked to the drug trade. This includes providing specialized training to police officers and prosecutors, as well as investing in advanced technologies and intelligence-sharing mechanisms to support their efforts.

The UAE's efforts to combat the economic implications of the drug trade, such as money laundering and corruption, are crucial not only for maintaining the integrity of its financial system and institutions but also for preserving its international reputation as a stable and secure business environment. However, the ever-evolving nature of the drug trade and its associated risks necessitate continuous vigilance and a comprehensive approach to effectively address these challenges.

3.   Counter-Narcotics Efforts

The UAE has implemented a variety of anti-narcotics measures in response to the growing threat that the drug trade poses to its society and economy. These measures encompass law enforcement initiatives, legislative and regulatory efforts, and demand reduction and treatment programs. In this article, we discuss each of these measures in greater detail and explore how they contribute to the UAE's comprehensive approach to combating the drug trade.

a. Law Enforcement: The UAE has significantly increased its law enforcement capacity to combat drug trafficking by investing in training, equipment, and intelligence-sharing initiatives to enhance the effectiveness of its anti-narcotics efforts (UNODC, 2016). The nation has established specialized counter-narcotics units within its police force, tasked with detecting, investigating, and dismantling drug trafficking networks. These specialized units are supported by advanced technologies, such as surveillance equipment and forensic tools, which enable them to conduct more efficient and effective operations.

In addition to bolstering its domestic law enforcement capabilities, the UAE has also engaged in cross-border cooperation with neighboring countries to disrupt drug trafficking networks (Hutchings & Guala, 2017). This cooperation includes joint operations, intelligence sharing, and capacity-building initiatives aimed at strengthening regional counter-narcotics efforts. By working closely with its neighbors, the UAE is better positioned to tackle the transnational nature of the drug trade and dismantle the criminal networks that operate across national borders.

b. Legislation and Regulation: The UAE has enacted strict anti-drug legislation, imposing severe penalties for drug trafficking, possession, and use (UAE Penal Code, 1987). These penalties serve as a deterrent for potential traffickers and users, signaling the government's commitment to combating the drug trade. In addition to its anti-drug legislation, the UAE has strengthened its anti-money laundering (AML) and counter-terrorism financing (CTF) regulations to combat the financial aspects of the drug trade (FATF, 2020). As discussed earlier, these regulations require financial institutions to maintain robust compliance programs and report suspicious transactions, helping to prevent the proceeds of drug trafficking from entering the UAE's financial system.

c. Demand Reduction and Treatment: The UAE has recognized the importance of addressing the demand side of the drug trade and has implemented a range of prevention and treatment programs to combat drug addiction within its borders (Alhyas et al., 2015). These initiatives include public awareness campaigns aimed at educating the population about the dangers of drug use and promoting healthy lifestyles. The UAE government also supports school-based education programs that teach students about the risks associated with drug use and equip them with the skills to resist peer pressure.

In addition to prevention efforts, the UAE has established specialized treatment centers for drug users (WHO, 2019). These centers provide comprehensive care and support for individuals struggling with addiction, offering a range of services such as detoxification, counseling, and medication-assisted treatment. The UAE government demonstrates its commitment to assisting those who are suffering from drug addiction and lowering the demand for illegal drugs within its borders by investing in these facilities.

The drug trade in the UAE is a complex and multifaceted issue, involving a range of local and international actors and posing significant challenges for the nation's society and economy. Addressing this problem requires a comprehensive and coordinated approach that encompasses law enforcement, legislation, regulation, and demand reduction measures. By investing in these efforts, the UAE can continue to combat the drug trade and minimize its impact on the nation's ongoing growth and development.

While the UAE's counter-narcotics strategy demonstrates a multifaceted approach that aims to yield positive results in the fight against drug trafficking and its associated consequences, it is essential to critically examine the efficacy of these efforts. The nation's investment in law enforcement, legislative and regulatory efforts, and demand reduction and treatment programs showcases its commitment to addressing the drug trade from multiple angles. However, the effectiveness of these measures in reducing drug trafficking and related organized crime remains a subject of ongoing debate (UNODC, 2016).

The UAE's law enforcement efforts, including the establishment of specialized anti-drug units and increased international cooperation, have led to several high-profile arrests and drug seizures (Europol, 2020). However, critics argue that the country's law enforcement agencies face significant challenges in terms of capacity, resources, and corruption. These factors may hinder their ability to effectively combat drug trafficking and dismantle organized crime networks (Shelley, 2014).

Moreover, while the UAE has enacted comprehensive legislative and regulatory frameworks to criminalize drug trafficking and money laundering, gaps remain in terms of implementation and enforcement. For instance, there have been concerns about the UAE's commitment to tackling money laundering and terrorist financing, as reflected in its placement on the FATF's "grey list" in 2020 (FATF, 2020). Furthermore, the UAE's legal framework has been criticized for its harsh penalties for drug offenses, which may disproportionately impact low-level offenders and non-violent drug users rather than targeting high-level traffickers and organized crime leaders (Human Rights Watch, 2019).

In terms of demand reduction and treatment programs, the UAE has taken steps to develop a more balanced and evidence-based approach to drug policy. This includes investing in public awareness campaigns, drug prevention programs, and harm reduction initiatives such as drug treatment and rehabilitation services (UNODC, 2016). However, critics argue that these efforts may be insufficient to address the underlying social, economic, and cultural factors that contribute to drug use and addiction in the country (Shelley, 2014).

To summarize, while the UAE's counter-narcotics strategy highlights its commitment to addressing drug trafficking and its associated consequences through a multifaceted approach, it is essential to critically evaluate the effectiveness of these efforts. Addressing the challenges faced by law enforcement agencies, closing gaps in the legislative and regulatory frameworks, and ensuring that demand reduction and treatment programs are adequately resourced and evidence-based are crucial steps towards achieving meaningful progress in the fight against drug trafficking and organized crime in the UAE.

THE MAFIA'S PRESENCE IN THE UAE

A. Key Mafia Groups and Their Activities

1. Overview

The United Arab Emirates (UAE) has experienced rapid economic growth in recent years, driven by its thriving business environment, strategic location, and robust infrastructure. While this growth has undoubtedly brought numerous benefits to the country, it has also attracted the attention of various mafia organizations looking to expand their operations and exploit the nation's lucrative markets (Galeotti, 2017). These groups have managed to establish a foothold in the UAE, engaging in a range of criminal activities, including money laundering, financial crimes, and human trafficking (Shelley, 2014).

2. Notable Mafia Groups

Some of the most prominent mafia organizations active in the UAE include:

a. Irish and Italian Mafia: The Italian Mafia, comprising several distinct criminal organizations such as the Sicilian Cosa Nostra, the Calabrian 'Ndrangheta, and the Neapolitan Camorra, has established a presence in the UAE, primarily focusing on money laundering and financial crimes (Galeotti, 2017). These groups often use the UAE's advanced financial infrastructure and its free trade zones to launder the proceeds of their criminal activities, invest in legitimate businesses, and establish front companies (Al Tamimi & Company, 2018).

The Italian mafia's presence in the UAE is not limited to money laundering and drug trafficking; it also extends to other forms of criminal activity such as arms smuggling, human trafficking, and counterfeiting (Global Initiative, 2018). The mafia's involvement in these activities highlights the extent of their influence and the potential threats they pose to the UAE's society, economy, and security.

The UAE, with its strategic location, strong economy, and growing international connections, has become an attractive destination for various organized crime groups, including the Italian mafia (Shelley, 2014). The presence of Italian mafia groups, such as the Cosa Nostra, the Camorra, and the 'Ndrangheta, in the UAE is primarily driven by their interest in exploiting the nation's financial system and infrastructure for money laundering and other criminal activities (Global Initiative, 2018).

Money laundering is a key concern when discussing the Italian mafia's activities in the UAE. The country's free trade zones, numerous financial institutions, and lax regulatory environment provide ample opportunities for mafia groups to launder their illicit proceeds, often through complex and interconnected business structures (Carnegie Endowment, 2020). Moreover, the UAE's growing real estate market has become a popular avenue for Italian mafia groups to launder their money, as property transactions are often used to legitimize the origin of illicit funds (Middle East Eye, 2021).

In addition to money laundering, the Italian mafia has also been linked to drug trafficking in the UAE. Mafia groups are known to use the UAE as a transit point for smuggling narcotics from producer countries, such as Afghanistan and Pakistan, to consumer markets in Europe and North America (UNODC, 2016). The UAE's well-developed transportation infrastructure, including its ports and airports, facilitates the movement of illicit goods, making it an attractive hub for drug traffickers (Hutchings & Guala, 2017).

To counter the presence and activities of the Italian mafia in the UAE, the country must strengthen its anti-money laundering (AML) and counter-terrorism financing (CTF) frameworks. This includes enhancing the capacity of law enforcement and regulatory agencies to detect, investigate, and prosecute money laundering cases, as well as improving coordination and information sharing among relevant authorities (FATF, 2020).

The UAE government has recognized the need to address organized crime, including the activities of the Italian mafia, and has taken several steps to combat this issue. The UAE has implemented measures to regulate its real estate sector, which the mafia has exploited for money laundering purposes, in addition to strengthening its AML/CTF framework and enhancing international cooperation (Carnegie Endowment, 2020).

Despite these efforts, the Italian mafia remains a persistent threat in the UAE. Continued vigilance and targeted action are necessary to dismantle these criminal networks and disrupt their operations. As the UAE continues to grow as a global hub, it must remain committed to addressing organized crime and safeguarding its stability, prosperity, and international reputation.

Raffaele Imperiale, a notorious member of the Camorra mafia and a fugitive drug boss, was extradited from Dubai to Italy in August 2021 (Gangsters Inc., 2021). Imperiale's arrest and extradition highlight the presence and activities of Italian organized crime in the United Arab Emirates (UAE), particularly in Dubai, which has become an attractive destination for members of various mafia groups seeking to expand their operations and evade law enforcement.

Imperiale was a leading figure in the Camorra, a powerful Italian mafia organization based in the Naples region. He was involved in the international drug trade, specifically in the trafficking of cocaine from South America to Europe (Gangsters Inc., 2021). According to Italian authorities, Imperiale was the mastermind behind a vast network that smuggled large quantities of cocaine from South America to Europe, using the UAE as a transit hub (UNODC, 2016).

Daniel Kinahan, an Irish mobster, has garnered significant attention for his activities in the United Arab Emirates (UAE), particularly in Dubai, where he has been residing for several years (MacNamee, 2020). Kinahan is widely believed to be the head of the Kinahan organized crime group, which has been involved in international drug trafficking, arms smuggling, and various other criminal activities (The Irish Times, 2021).

The Kinahan crime group has its origins in Ireland, but over time, it has expanded its operations and influence across Europe, particularly in Spain and the Netherlands, as well as in the UAE (Connolly, 2020). Daniel Kinahan's presence in Dubai has raised concerns about the UAE's role as a haven for organized crime figures and the potential for criminal networks to exploit the country's strategic location, lax investment laws, and growing wealth (Hutchings & Guala, 2017).

Kinahan's activities in the UAE have been widely reported in the media, particularly in relation to his involvement in the boxing industry. He has been instrumental in brokering high-profile boxing deals and establishing relationships with prominent figures in the sport, despite ongoing investigations into his alleged criminal activities (The Guardian, 2020). This has led to calls for greater scrutiny of Kinahan's involvement in boxing and his connections to organized crime.

b. Russian Mafia: Drawn by the UAE's expanding wealth and opportunities for money laundering and other illegal activities, the Russian Mafia, also known as the "Bratva," has expanded its operations there (Galeotti, 2017). These organizations are involved in various criminal enterprises, including drug trafficking, arms smuggling, and human trafficking (Shelley, 2014).

The author of the article "Dubai Emerges as a Russian Oligarch Safe Haven Amid the Ukraine War" (The New York Times, 2023) examines the role of Dubai as a sanctuary for wealthy Russian oligarchs seeking to avoid the economic fallout and political scrutiny that resulted from Russia's invasion of Ukraine. The article is titled "Dubai Emerges as a Russian Oligarch Safe Haven Amid the Ukraine War." The article addresses the difficulties that the UAE faces in preserving its neutrality and reputation as a global financial hub while addressing concerns about money laundering and illegal financial flows. Specifically, the essay focuses on the difficulties that the UAE faces in maintaining its reputation.

According to the author of an article that was published in The New York Times (2023), many Russian oligarchs have migrated to Dubai as a result of the implementation of international sanctions on Russia as a result of its activities in Ukraine. These people are lured to the emirate because of its advantageous tax climate, political stability, and opulent lifestyle options. Concerns have been expressed over the possibility of money laundering as well as the effect that this phenomenon may have on the UAE's position in the international community as a result of the influx of riches from Russia into Dubai.

According to the article published in The New York Times (2023), the United Arab Emirates has remained impartial in the confrontation between Russia and Ukraine despite the fact that it has provided safe haven to Russian oligarchs and their families. Some Western countries have criticized this strategy, arguing that the UAE's acceptance of Russian riches may undermine efforts to persuade Moscow to stop its aggressive behavior in Ukraine. These countries think that the UAE's welcoming of Russian wealth may undermine efforts to pressure Moscow into ceasing its aggression in Ukraine. According to the information presented in the article, the United Arab Emirates' policy toward Russian oligarchs may be motivated by economic concerns as well as a desire to strike a balance in its connections with important world powers.

(The New York Times, 2023) The author also addresses the potential ramifications of the UAE's attitude toward its status as a worldwide financial hub. The sudden rush of riches from Russia into Dubai has prompted some to question the efficiency of anti-money laundering and counter-terrorism funding measures implemented by the United Arab Emirates (UAE). The article expresses worry that the United Arab Emirates (UAE) might come under more scrutiny from international organizations like the Financial Action Task Force (FATF) if it fails to appropriately address the issues that have been raised.

The article highlights the difficulties encountered by the UAE in navigating the complicated geopolitical environment as a direct result of the conflict that has been going on between Russia and Ukraine (The New York Times, 2023). In addition to preserving its neutrality and guarding its own interests, the emirate must also address issues over money laundering and the flow of illegal funds if it is to maintain its status as a global financial hub. This involves upgrading its regulatory system, working more closely with foreign partners, and displaying a dedication to the fight against financial crime.

c. Balkan Organized Crime: Organized crime groups from the Balkans, including the Albanian, Serbian, and Montenegrin mafias, have also established a presence in the UAE, exploiting the nation's strategic location and global connectivity to expand their criminal networks (Europol, 2018).

In the article "Balkan Criminals Find a Home in the UAE and the Gulf" (Global Initiative Against Transnational Organized Crime, n.d.), the author discusses the increasing presence of Balkan organized crime groups in the United Arab Emirates (UAE) and other Gulf countries. The article highlights the factors attracting these criminals to the region, the activities they are engaged in, and the challenges faced by local law enforcement in combating this growing threat.

The author explains that the UAE, particularly Dubai, has become a popular destination for Balkan criminal groups due to its strategic location, business-friendly environment, and lax financial regulations (Global Initiative Against Transnational Organized Crime, n.d.). These factors, combined with the UAE's attractive lifestyle and perceived safety, have made the country an ideal base for criminals seeking to expand their operations, launder money, and evade law enforcement in their home countries.

The article also notes that Balkan criminals in the UAE are involved in a range of illicit activities, including drug trafficking, money laundering, and fraud (Global Initiative Against Transnational Organized Crime, n.d.). The author cites cases of Balkan criminal networks working with local and international partners to facilitate the smuggling of narcotics, as well as using the UAE's free trade zones and real estate sector to launder the proceeds of their crimes.

Furthermore, the article discusses the challenges faced by local law enforcement in the UAE in combating the activities of Balkan criminal groups (Global Initiative Against Transnational Organized Crime, n.d.). These challenges include the lack of bilateral extradition treaties between the UAE and some Balkan countries, the limited capacity of local law enforcement agencies to gather intelligence on foreign criminal networks, and the difficulty of tracking the complex financial transactions used to launder illicit proceeds.

The author also emphasizes the importance of international cooperation in addressing the issue of Balkan organized crime in the UAE and the Gulf region (Global Initiative Against Transnational Organized Crime, n.d.). This includes sharing intelligence and resources between countries, as well as working together to strengthen legal frameworks and improve law enforcement capabilities. The article also highlights the need for the UAE and other Gulf countries to adopt more stringent financial regulations and anti-money laundering measures to prevent their territories from being exploited by criminal networks.

In summary, the article underscores the growing presence of Balkan organized crime groups in the UAE and the Gulf region, driven by the area's strategic location, business-friendly environment, and permissive financial regulations (Global Initiative Against Transnational Organized Crime, n.d.). The author calls for enhanced international cooperation and the strengthening of local law enforcement capabilities to address this threat effectively and prevent the region from becoming a safe haven for criminals.

d. Indian and Pakistani Mafia:

Indian and Pakistani mafia groups have established a significant presence in the UAE, exploiting the country's strategic location, business-friendly environment, and large expatriate communities from the Indian subcontinent. Their activities in the UAE include drug trafficking, money laundering, human trafficking, and organized crime-related violence (Shelley, 2014).

Dawood Ibrahim, the infamous underworld figure and mastermind behind the D-Company crime syndicate, has had a long-standing connection with Dubai, the most populous city in the United Arab Emirates (UAE) (Jamwal, 2001). Over the years, Ibrahim has used the city as a base for his criminal operations, leveraging Dubai's strategic location, thriving economy, and lax regulatory environment to further his illegal activities (Lokhande, 2019).

Dawood Ibrahim is said to have built a foothold in Dubai throughout the late 1980s and early 1990s. According to Jamwal (2001), Dawood Ibrahim had various properties and enterprises in Dubai. During this time, he broadened the scope of the D-Company's operations to include a variety of illegal pursuits, such as drug trafficking, extortion, money laundering, and arms smuggling. Because of his power in Dubai, he was able to form connections with other international criminal organizations, which helped to further expand the D-Company's presence across the world (Lokhande, 2019).

According to Jamwal (2001), one of the primary reasons that Dawood Ibrahim decided to settle in Dubai was because of the city's rapidly expanding economy and its reputation as a developing center for international commerce and finance. Because of this atmosphere, there were many chances for money laundering, as the D-Company was able to readily abuse Dubai's financial system and enter legitimate firms in order to launder the proceeds of their illegal operations (Lokhande, 2019). In addition, because of Dubai's strategic location between East and West, it has become an excellent transit point for the trafficking of drugs as well as other forms of illegal commerce (Jamwal, 2001).

However, beginning in the late 1990s, the presence of Dawood Ibrahim in Dubai began to attract the attention of international law enforcement agencies. As a result, the government of the UAE came under increased scrutiny and pressure to take action against him (Jamwal, 2001). As a direct consequence of this, Ibrahim relocated his base of operations to Karachi, Pakistan, where he is thought to be staying under the protection of the government of Pakistan (Lokhande, 2019).

In spite of the fact that he moved out of the city, Dawood Ibrahim's influence in Dubai has survived through the network of accomplices and front firms that he established there (Lokhande, 2019). The actions of the D-Company in Dubai continue to be a significant source of worry for law enforcement authorities since these activities contribute to the growth of organized crime and present a risk to the city's stability and reputation (Jamwal, 2001).

Drug Trafficking: The UAE's proximity to the Golden Crescent, a major opium-producing region encompassing Afghanistan, Iran, and Pakistan, has made it an attractive transit point for drug traffickers (UNODC, 2016). Indian and Pakistani mafia groups are involved in smuggling narcotics, such as heroin and hashish, through the UAE and onwards to consumer markets in Europe, North America, and Africa (Europol, 2020).

Dubai, with its strategic location and status as a global trade hub, has long been a hotspot for drug trafficking activities. Criminal networks, particularly those from India and Pakistan, have increasingly exploited Dubai's free trade zones and lax regulations to facilitate the illicit drug trade (Gupta & Raghavan, 2020).

Indian and Pakistani drug traffickers have primarily focused on smuggling narcotics such as heroin, opium, and synthetic drugs through Dubai enroute to international markets, including Europe and North America (Gupta & Raghavan, 2020). These traffickers often use sophisticated methods to conceal their contraband, such as hiding drugs within legal shipments or employing drug mules who smuggle narcotics in their luggage or body cavities (UNODC, 2016).

A significant factor contributing to the presence of Indian and Pakistani drug traffickers in Dubai is the historical and cultural ties between the UAE and the South Asian region (Morrison, 2018). The large South Asian expatriate population in Dubai provides a cover for drug traffickers to blend into the community, making it easier for them to evade detection by law enforcement agencies (Morrison, 2018).

One high-profile example of Indian and Pakistani drug trafficking activities in Dubai is the case of the D-Company, a notorious criminal organization led by Dawood Ibrahim, which has been implicated in several drug smuggling operations in the region (Jamwal, 2001). The D-Company has reportedly established a network of local and international collaborators, including Afghan and Iranian drug traffickers, to facilitate the movement of narcotics through Dubai (Jamwal, 2001).

Money Laundering: Indian and Pakistani criminal networks utilize the UAE's financial system and free trade zones to launder proceeds from their illicit activities (FATF, 2020). They may employ various money laundering techniques, including the use of shell companies, front businesses, and informal money transfer systems such as hawala (Hutchings & Guala, 2017).

Indian and Pakistani money laundering activities in the United Arab Emirates (UAE), particularly in Dubai, have become a significant concern in recent years. The UAE's status as a major global financial hub, combined with its relaxed regulations and free trade zones, has made it an attractive destination for money launderers from these South Asian countries (U.S. Department of State, 2020).

Indian and Pakistani money launderers use various methods to conceal the origins of illicit funds and integrate them into the legitimate financial system. These techniques include trade-based money laundering (TBML), which involves over- or under-invoicing of goods and services, as well as round-tripping, where funds are moved offshore and then returned as foreign direct investment (FDI) (FATF, 2020). Additionally, money launderers exploit the UAE's real estate market, using it as a vehicle to launder proceeds from illegal activities such as drug trafficking, corruption, and tax evasion (Middle East Eye, 2018).

The involvement of politically exposed persons (PEPs) from India and Pakistan in money laundering schemes in the UAE has also been a notable issue. In 2018, the Pakistani Supreme Court disqualified former Prime Minister Nawaz Sharif from holding public office due to his family's undisclosed assets in Dubai (Al Jazeera, 2018). Similarly, Indian authorities have been investigating high-profile individuals, including fugitive businessman Nirav Modi, who allegedly laundered money through UAE-based companies (The Hindu, 2020).

To combat Indian and Pakistani money laundering in the UAE, the government has taken steps to strengthen its anti-money laundering

(AML) and counter-terrorist financing (CTF) frameworks. In 2020, the UAE introduced the Economic Substance Regulations, which require companies to demonstrate real economic activity within the country to prevent the misuse of corporate structures for money laundering purposes (UAE Ministry of Finance, 2020). The UAE has also joined the Egmont Group, an international organization that facilitates information sharing among financial intelligence units (FIUs) to combat money laundering and terrorist financing (Egmont Group, 2020).

Despite these efforts, challenges remain in addressing Indian and Pakistani money laundering in the UAE. A key issue is the lack of transparency in the UAE's beneficial ownership information, which enables money launderers to conceal their identities behind complex corporate structures (FATF, 2020). The UAE must also enhance its cooperation with Indian and Pakistani authorities to facilitate the exchange of information and coordinate joint investigations into money laundering cases (FATF, 2020).

Human Trafficking: Indian and Pakistani mafia groups are also involved in human trafficking operations in the UAE, exploiting vulnerable individuals from their home countries for forced labor or sexual exploitation (ILO, 2018). These criminal networks often use fraudulent recruitment practices and debt bondage to control their victims and profit from their exploitation (US Department of State, 2020).

Human trafficking is a global problem that affects millions of people, and the UAE is no exception. Indian and Pakistani nationals are among those vulnerable to human trafficking, particularly in the UAE, where they constitute a significant percentage of the expatriate workforce (Khan & Webb, 2018). Human trafficking in the UAE involving Indian and Pakistani nationals often takes the form of forced labor, sexual exploitation, and domestic servitude (US Department of State, 2021).

The kafala system, which governs the employment of migrant workers in the UAE, has been widely criticized for facilitating human trafficking as it ties workers' legal status to their employers (Baldwin-

Edwards, 2011). This system leaves Indian and Pakistani workers vulnerable to exploitation, as they are often trapped in abusive situations with limited recourse to seek help or change employers (Human Rights Watch, 2020).

To address human trafficking involving Indian and Pakistani nationals in the UAE, it is crucial to strengthen the existing legal framework and ensure its effective implementation. This includes revising labor laws to provide better protection for migrant workers, particularly those in vulnerable sectors such as construction and domestic work (US Department of State, 2021). Additionally, the UAE should consider abolishing the kafala system and replacing it with a more equitable system that grants workers greater freedom and mobility (Human Rights Watch, 2020).

Law enforcement and judicial authorities in the UAE must also be better equipped to identify, investigate, and prosecute human trafficking cases involving Indian and Pakistani nationals. This includes providing specialized training, resources, and support to strengthen their capacity to address human trafficking crimes (US Department of State, 2021).

Furthermore, the UAE should enhance cooperation with Indian and Pakistani authorities in the fight against human trafficking. This includes sharing information, intelligence, and best practices to facilitate the identification, investigation, and prosecution of trafficking networks, as well as the repatriation and reintegration of victims (US Department of State, 2021).

Public awareness campaigns are another essential component of addressing human trafficking involving Indian and Pakistani nationals in the UAE. By educating the public about the signs and consequences of human trafficking, the UAE can encourage the reporting of suspected cases and foster a culture of vigilance and support for victims (US Department of State, 2021).

Organized Crime-Related Violence: The presence of Indian and Pakistani mafia groups in the UAE has been linked to incidents of violence, as these criminal networks vie for control of lucrative illicit markets (Shelley, 2014). In some cases, mafia-related violence has targeted rival gang members or law enforcement personnel, posing a threat to public safety in the UAE (Chatterjee, 2018).

One of the most trusted associates of Dawood Ibrahim, an infamous figure in the Indian underworld who was also sought for terrorism, was killed in Dubai in May of 2014. This event brought to light the presence of Indian mafia organizations in the United Arab Emirates (UAE) as well as the activities that they engage in (Times of India, 2014).

Dawood Ibrahim, the ringleader of the D-Company criminal organization and the person most responsible for the explosions that occurred in Mumbai in 1993, has been on India's most-wanted list for many years. His group is involved in a wide range of illegal pursuits, including the trafficking of illegal drugs and firearms as well as the laundering of illicit funds. Iqbal Mirchi, who worked for Ibrahim, was shot and murdered in Dubai in what is believed to have been a gang-related incident. This incident highlights the constant competition and violence that exist amongst criminal groups operating within the UAE (Times of India, 2014).

Because of their advantageous location, business-friendly atmosphere, and comparatively lenient law enforcement, the United Arab Emirates and Dubai in particular have become refuges for criminal organizations hailing from India and Pakistan. Worries have been expressed regarding the possible impact that these organized criminal organizations in the UAE might have on the country's security, economic stability, and social stability (Times of India, 2014). These groups' presence in the UAE has generated these worries.

Mafia organizations continue to operate within the UAE despite the efforts that have been made by the UAE government to combat organized crime. These groups make use of the country's financial and commerce infrastructure in order to launder money and enable illegal operations. According to the Times of India (2014), the assassination of Ibrahim's assistant in Dubai highlights the necessity for more effective steps to confront the rising danger presented by organized crime in the UAE.

In addition, the existence of mafia organizations from India and Pakistan in the United Arab Emirates has called into question the efficacy of international collaboration in the fight against transnational organized crime. According to the Times of India (2014), the inability of law enforcement officials in the area to capture Dawood Ibrahim and destroy his criminal network underscores the obstacles encountered by law enforcement agencies in the region.

The assassination of an assistant to Dawood Ibrahim in Dubai in 2014 sheds light on the presence of Indian and Pakistani mafia groups in the UAE as well as the operations they engage in there. This episode highlights the necessity for more rigorous measures to combat organized crime and to increase international collaboration in order to guarantee the security and stability of the area (Times of India, 2014).

B. Money Laundering and Financial Crimes

1. Money Laundering

Mafia organizations operating in the United Arab Emirates (UAE) are heavily involved in money laundering activities, seeking to legitimize the proceeds of their criminal enterprises by funneling them through the nation's financial system (FATF, 2020). The UAE's advanced banking sector, ease of doing business, and numerous free trade zones make it an attractive destination for money launderers (Al Tamimi & Company, 2018).

Attractiveness of the UAE for Money Laundering

Advanced Banking Sector: The UAE's well-developed banking sector, featuring sophisticated financial products and services, offers a conducive environment for money laundering activities. The presence of numerous international banks and financial institutions provides organized crime groups with ample opportunities to obscure the origin of their illicit funds and integrate them into the legitimate financial system.

Ease of Doing Business: The UAE is known for its business-friendly environment, characterized by minimal bureaucracy, streamlined registration processes, and low taxation. This ease of doing business allows mafia organizations to set up shell companies and other legal entities that can be used to launder their ill-gotten gains without raising suspicion.

Free Trade Zones: The UAE is home to several free trade zones that offer numerous incentives to businesses, such as tax exemptions, 100% foreign ownership, and relaxed import and export regulations. These free trade zones provide an ideal setting for money launderers to establish front companies, which can be used to move funds across borders and disguise the origin of their criminal proceeds.

2.   Methods of Money Laundering

Mafia groups use a variety of methods to launder money in the UAE, including:

a. Real Estate: Mafia organizations often invest in the UAE's real estate market, purchasing high-end properties and luxury developments to launder their criminal proceeds (Galeotti, 2017).

The author of the piece titled "Dubai: How foreigners are laundering billions through UAE real estate" (Middle East Eye, n.d.) analyzes the function of the real estate market in the United Arab Emirates (UAE), and more specifically in Dubai, as a vehicle for the laundering of money by international criminals. The essay focuses on the characteristics that make the real estate industry in the UAE an appealing location for illegal financial operations as well as the problems that the UAE authorities confront in attempting to combat this issue.

According to the author of an article published in Middle East Eye (n.d.), Dubai's thriving real estate market, along with the UAE's business-friendly atmosphere and loose financial rules, has turned the country into a magnet for international criminals looking to launder the proceeds of their illegal operations. According to the information presented in the article, the real estate industry in the UAE is especially susceptible to the practice of money laundering owing to the absence of transparency in property ownership, the simplicity of moving huge quantities of money, and the lack of control over financial transactions.

This article presents numerous examples of high-profile cases involving foreign people and businesses laundering money through the real estate market in the UAE (Middle East Eye, n.d.). The cases included real estate transactions in the United Arab Emirates. These instances illustrate the scope and complexity of the problem, as well as the difficulties that local and international law enforcement organizations encounter when attempting to hunt down and prosecute those participating in illegal activity.

In addition, the author stresses the need for the United Arab Emirates (UAE) to strengthen its anti-money laundering (AML) legislation and increase the transparency of its real estate sector in order to reduce the amount of illegal cash entering the nation (Middle East Eye, n.d.). This is done in order to stop the flow of illicit funds into the country. According to the information presented in the article, the United Arab Emirates ought to strengthen its collaboration with foreign law enforcement agencies, embrace worldwide best practices in AML compliance, and implement more strict due diligence methods for property transactions.

(Middle East Eye, n.d.) The piece also explores the larger ramifications of money laundering in the UAE's real estate industry for the economy and prestige of the country. The author contends that the entry of illegal funds into the real estate market in the UAE might distort market pricing, promote speculation, and jeopardize the stability of the financial system in that nation. In addition, the author of the essay expresses concerns that if the United Arab Emirates (UAE) does not properly combat money laundering in its real estate market, it may suffer a blow to its reputation on the world stage and be subject to economic consequences.

The article emphasizes the problems brought about by international criminals' extensive use of the real estate market in the UAE, particularly in Dubai, as a conduit for money laundering (Middle East Eye, n.d.). The article focuses in particular on the difficulties brought about by the widespread use of the Dubai real estate market. In order to properly handle this problem and defend the economy and prestige of the country, the author urges the United Arab Emirates to tighten its anti-money laundering rules, increase the transparency of its property sector, and expand collaboration with foreign law enforcement organizations.

b. Front Companies: Mafia groups also establish front companies in the UAE's free trade zones, using these entities to move funds and launder money through seemingly legitimate business transactions (Al Tamimi & Company, 2018).

The author of the article "How the UAE helps Putin's cronies avoid sanctions" (Pravda, 2022) investigates the role that the United Arab Emirates (UAE) plays in facilitating the evasion of international sanctions that have been imposed on Russian oligarchs and Putin's associates as a result of Russia's aggressive actions in Ukraine. The sanctions have been imposed as a result of Russia's involvement in the conflict in Ukraine. The report underlines the UAE's geopolitical location, financial infrastructure, and legal framework, all of which make it an appealing destination for Russian people and businesses that are attempting to dodge these sanctions.

According to what the author says in Pravda (2022), the United Arab Emirates has become a favorite location for Russian firms and people who want to protect their assets from the impact of western sanctions. The country's free trade zones create a conducive environment for Russian organizations to form shell companies and conduct financial transactions without drawing the notice of foreign regulators because they grant tax exemptions and loosen financial restrictions. This environment is beneficial for Russian firms because it allows Russian entities to avoid catching the attention of international regulators.

The article also makes the point that the United Arab Emirates' (UAE) lack of transparency in financial transactions, in addition to its lax rules for anti-money laundering (AML), contributes to its attractiveness as a center for Russian people and businesses wanting to circumvent sanctions (Pravda, 2022). The author adds that the UAE's authorities have been sluggish in applying international AML rules, which has made it easier for sanctioned individuals and organizations to conduct business in the country. In addition, the author says that this has resulted in a lack of transparency in the UAE's financial system.

In addition, the article explores the role those financial institutions in the UAE, notably its banks, play in easing the transfer of cash for Russian people and organizations (Pravda, 2022). The author discusses many incidents in which UAE-based banks have been implicated in transactions with Russian firms that are subject to sanctions. These cases raise issues about the efficiency of the UAE's financial monitoring as well as its commitment to implementing international sanctions (Pravda, 2022).

The author places a strong emphasis on the necessity for the United Arab Emirates (UAE) to enhance its regulatory framework and increase its implementation of international sanctions in order to prevent Russian billionaires and Putin's allies from using the UAE's financial system. According to the information presented in the article, in order for the United Arab Emirates to properly solve this matter, the country ought to implement more strict AML measures, boost the transparency of financial transactions, and enhance coordination with international regulatory authorities.

This article also analyzes the larger ramifications of the United Arab Emirates' participation in supporting the evasion of sanctions for the international community as well as the effectiveness of sanctions as a weapon for policymaking (Pravda, 2022). The author contends that the United Arab Emirates' (UAE's) failure to adequately enforce international sanctions undermines the global effort to hold Russia accountable for its actions in Ukraine and sends a signal to other countries that they can exploit the gaps in the international sanction's regime for their own benefit. Additionally, the failure of the UAE to adequately enforce international sanctions sends a signal that Russia will not be held accountable for its actions in Ukraine.

The article focuses on the challenges posed by the UAE's assistance to Russian billionaires and Putin allies in evading international sanctions (Pravda, 2022). To ensure the efficiency of the global sanctions system and to assist efforts to hold Russia responsible for its activities in Ukraine, the author urges the United Arab Emirates to improve its enforcement of sanctions, strengthen its regulatory framework, and boost its collaboration with international organizations. This would help to ensure that the global sanctions regime is efficient.

c. Trade-Based Money Laundering: Mafia organizations exploit the UAE's extensive trade networks to engage in trade-based money laundering, over- or under-invoicing goods and services to move funds across borders and obscure the origins of their criminal proceeds (FATF, 2020).

The results of research that was carried out by the Bureau for International Narcotics and Law Enforcement Affairs of the United States Department of State are discussed in the piece entitled "Dubai: A Haven for Trade-Based Money Laundering, Tells US Study" (AML Newsflow, 2020). In this piece, the author examines the conclusions of the study. According to the findings of the study, Dubai has developed a reputation as a center for trade-based money laundering (TBML) as a result of its advantageous location, broad trade networks, and relaxed regulatory environment.

The article outlines various aspects that contribute to Dubai's desirability as a hub for TBML, including its role as a global trade center and its free trade zones (AML Newsflow, 2020). Among these considerations is Dubai's attractiveness as a location for doing TBML business. Businesses that deal in TBML may find it beneficial to locate in one of the free trade zones in the UAE since these zones provide a variety of advantages, including tax exemptions and laxer financial requirements. These zones allow for the formation of front firms and the misrepresentation of commercial transactions, which provides criminals with the opportunity to clean dirty money through operations that give the appearance of being legal in nature.

In addition to this, the research highlights the role that lax anti-money laundering (AML) legislation and enforcement in Dubai play in making it possible for TBML (AML Newsflow, 2020). The United Arab Emirates has lagged behind other countries in terms of implementing international AML rules, and its governing bodies have had a difficult time successfully investigating and prosecuting TBML instances. The opaque nature of financial dealings and the lax regulation of the country's free trade zones are both contributing factors that make the problem even more difficult to solve.

According to the article, "Dubai's Role as a TBML Hub Has Significant Implications for the Global Financial System," because it enables criminals to leverage the city's trade networks in order to transport illegal funds across borders (AML Newsflow, 2020), This has substantial ramifications for the worldwide financial system. The efficiency of international efforts to combat money laundering is harmed as a result, and the security and reliability of the international financial system are put in danger.

The author places a strong emphasis on the necessity for Dubai to develop its regulatory framework, improve its AML enforcement, and improve its interaction with international partners in order to successfully handle the problem of TBML (AML Newsflow, 2020). According to the information presented in the article, the United Arab Emirates ought to implement more strict AML safeguards, raise the openness of its financial activities, and strengthen its ability to investigate and punish TBML instances.

In addition to this, the article stresses the role that the international community plays in supporting the efforts that Dubai is making to combat TBML (AML Newsflow, 2020). The author contends that more collaboration and information sharing between nations and international organizations is needed to detect and dismantle TBML networks, as well as to assure the efficacy of global efforts to combat money laundering.

The paper sheds light on Dubai's rising significance as a hub for trade-based money laundering (AML Newsflow, 2020). Dubai's strategic location, extensive trade networks, and lax regulatory environment are what are driving this growing prominence. In order to successfully handle this problem and maintain the integrity of the international financial system, the author urges the UAE to fortify its regulatory framework, increase its enforcement of anti-money laundering rules, and improve its collaboration with international partners.

3. Impact on the UAE's Economy

Money laundering activities by mafia organizations can have significant negative consequences for the UAE's economy, including:

a. Undermining Financial Integrity: Money laundering activities can compromise the integrity of the UAE's financial system, exposing the nation to reputational risks and potential sanctions from international organizations (IMF, 2017).

It is a serious problem that affects the financial integrity of the United Arab Emirates (UAE) by facilitating the flow of illegal monies through the economy of the nation. Money laundering does this by making it easier for criminals to get their hands on money. As a result of its fast expansion as a global financial hub, the United Arab Emirates (UAE) has become an attractive destination for criminals who are looking to launder money from a variety of unlawful operations (Hutchings & Guala, 2017). This is due to the UAE's strategic position as well as its permissive regulatory environment.

The compromising of the openness and accountability of financial transactions is one of the key ways that money laundering erodes financial integrity in the UAE. This is one of the primary ways that money laundering erodes financial integrity in the UAE. Criminals frequently use shell businesses to facilitate the flow of illegal money (Carnegie Endowment, 2020). These firms are created by taking advantage of the wide network of free trade zones that exist across the United States. These zones provide tax exemptions and loose financial laws. These shell corporations have the potential to obscure the genuine sources of money, making it more challenging for law enforcement to track down illegal assets and seize them.

In addition, the activity of money laundering has the potential to skew economic data and impair the robustness of the financial system in the UAE. According to Middle East Eye (2018), money laundering may cause asset bubbles and encourage hazardous investing behavior by artificially inflating the value of assets and enabling the transfer of illegal cash into legitimate ventures. This has the potential to ultimately bring about financial crises and worsen the state of the economy as a whole.

The prevalence of money laundering in the UAE may be detrimental to the country's worldwide reputation as well as its ties with important commercial partners. As a result of the United Arab Emirates being labeled as a jurisdiction with a high risk of money laundering by organizations such as the Financial Action Task Force (FATF), it is subject to a greater level of scrutiny from international regulators and financial institutions (FATF, 2020). This may lead to a decrease in foreign investment, an increase in the expenditures associated with compliance, and strained diplomatic relations.

It is essential for the United Arab Emirates (UAE) to tighten its anti-money laundering (AML) rules and enforcement if the country is going to tackle the problem of money laundering and defend its financial stability at the same time. This involves implementing international AML standards, raising the level of openness in financial transactions, and boosting the capacity of law enforcement authorities to investigate and punish incidents of money laundering (AML Newsflow, 2020).

In addition, in order to successfully combat money laundering, the United Arab Emirates has to increase its cooperation with foreign partners. This requires increased coordination and information sharing between nations and international organizations (Shelley, 2014). The goal is to identify and destroy criminal networks that are engaged in the practice of money laundering.

The facilitation of the movement of illegal cash, the compromise of the transparency of financial transactions, and the weakening of the stability of the economy are all key ways in which money laundering poses a substantial danger to the financial integrity of the UAE. The United Arab Emirates needs to tighten its regulatory framework, improve its enforcement of anti-money laundering rules, and increase its collaboration with foreign partners in order to successfully handle this issue and protect the nation's financial integrity.

b. Distorting Economic Activity: The influx of illicit funds into the UAE's economy can distort economic activity, artificially inflating asset prices and undermining the stability of financial markets (FATF, 2020).

Laundering illicit funds is a prevalent problem that skews economic activity in the United Arab Emirates (UAE). As a result, it has an effect on a number of components of the UAE's financial system as well as the nation's general economic health. According to Unger and Busuioc (2007), the act of money laundering is the process of integrating illegal funds into the normal economy. This makes it difficult for authorities to detect and track these funds. As will be seen in the following discussion, this approach has a number of unfavorable repercussions for the economy of the UAE.

To begin, the act of laundering money might result in the inappropriate distribution of resources within the economy. As criminals invest illegal funds in a variety of industries, they have the potential to create artificial demand for certain products and services. This has the effect of distorting market signals and leading to an inefficient distribution of resources (Unger, 2007). In consequence, this can limit economic progress and inhibit the development of an economy that is lively and diversified.

Second, the activity of money laundering has the potential to encourage the growth of asset bubbles. Criminals are able to push up asset values and generate bubbles that are not sustainable over the long term if they pump substantial quantities of illegal money into specialized industries, such as real estate (Unger, 2007). As was the case with the worldwide financial crisis that occurred in 2008, these bubbles, when they burst, can set off financial crises and economic downturns.

Third, the integrity and stability of the UAE's financial institutions are compromised when there is widespread money laundering. When criminals take advantage of flaws in the nation's financial system to launder money, they put banks and other financial institutions at risk of suffering losses as a result of the collapse of illicit organizations (Unger & Busuioc, 2007). These losses might include reputational harm, regulatory penalties, and possible losses caused by the failure of criminal companies. This, in turn, can have the effect of undermining faith in the financial system and discouraging legal firms and investors from participating in the economy of the UAE.

Fourth, financial inequality and social imbalances in the UAE may become even more pronounced as a result of money laundering. Money laundering may increase the gap between the affluent and the poor and establish a culture of corruption that perpetuates social and economic inequities (Unger, 2007). It does this by enabling criminals to amass large sums of wealth through illegal methods.

The United Arab Emirates (UAE) needs to tighten its anti-money laundering (AML) rules and enforcement systems in order to mitigate the detrimental consequences that money laundering has on the country's economy. This involves the adoption of international AML standards, the enhancement of openness in financial transactions, and the strengthening of the ability of law enforcement authorities to investigate and prosecute instances involving money laundering (Unger & Busuioc, 2007). In addition, the United Arab Emirates ought to strengthen its collaboration with foreign partners in order to more effectively tackle money laundering and other financial crimes.

Money laundering is an important problem that exacerbates income inequality, contributes to the creation of asset bubbles, undermines the stability of financial institutions, and causes economic activity in the UAE to be distorted. It does this by leading to the misallocation of resources, which in turn contributes to the construction of asset bubbles. The United Arab Emirates (UAE) needs to establish stringent anti-money laundering (AML) measures and create stronger international collaboration in the fight against financial crime in order to overcome these difficulties and support sustainable economic growth.

C. Human Trafficking and Prostitution

1. Human Trafficking & Prostitution

Mafia organizations operating in the UAE are also involved in human trafficking, exploiting the nation's strategic location and global connectivity to move victims across borders and profit from their exploitation (Europol, 2018). These groups typically target vulnerable individuals from economically disadvantaged countries, offering them false promises of employment and a better life in the UAE before subjecting them to forced labor, sexual exploitation, or other forms of modern slavery (Shelley, 2014).

The UAE has become a destination for sex trafficking and prostitution, with mafia organizations playing a significant role in facilitating these activities (Europol, 2018). These groups often operate brothels, massage parlors, and escort services, exploiting the victims of human trafficking and profiting from their sexual exploitation (Shelley, 2014).

Laundering illicit funds and trafficking in people are two forms of organized crime that are intricately linked to one another and represent serious risks to the health and safety of societies everywhere, including the United Arab Emirates (UAE). Both activities are motivated by the search for illegal riches, with human trafficking bringing in billions of dollars in income for criminal groups throughout the world (Dollar, 2014). This is the driving force behind both of these operations. In the United Arab Emirates, human trafficking and the connected crime of prostitution have been linked to the expansion of money laundering as criminals utilize the nation's financial system to launder the earnings of these horrible crimes (Rijken, 2011). In addition, money laundering has been linked to the growth of human trafficking.

One of the ways in which money laundering contributes to the problem of human trafficking and prostitution in the UAE is that it enables criminals to have access to the resources they need to launch and run their illegal businesses. According to Dollar (2014), criminal organizations rely on the profits made from human trafficking and prostitution in order to support their operations, which include the recruitment of victims, their transportation, and their abuse of them. By concealing the sources of their money and using it to develop their activities, criminals can further perpetuate the cycle of human trafficking and prostitution by laundering the proceeds of their crimes through the financial system of the UAE (Rijken, 2011).

Additionally, money laundering enables networks involved in human trafficking and prostitution to establish a facade of legitimacy, which can assist these networks in evading detection and prosecution by authorities in charge of law enforcement. Criminals can provide a cover for their actions and make it easier to abuse victims by investing the earnings they make from illegal activities in legitimate enterprises such as hotels, restaurants, or entertainment venues (Dollar, 2014). In turn, this makes it more difficult for the police to identify the criminal networks that are responsible for these crimes and dismantle them.

Because of the United Arab Emirates' rapid economic expansion and its position as a worldwide hub for commerce, tourism, and finance, the prevalence of human trafficking and prostitution in the country is also connected to these two factors. Because of the UAE's booming economy, there is a growing need for low-cost labor and commercial sex, both of which have drawn the attention of criminal organizations that are looking to make a profit off of the exploitation of vulnerable people (Rijken, 2011). In addition, the modern infrastructure and banking system of the UAE have made it possible for criminals to launder money made through human trafficking and prostitution, which has further exacerbated the situation.

The United Arab Emirates (UAE) needs to enhance its legal and regulatory frameworks, as well as its enforcement mechanisms, in order to address the ties between money laundering, human trafficking, and prostitution in the country. This includes the adoption of comprehensive anti-money laundering (AML) and anti-human trafficking legislation, the enhancement of the capability of law enforcement agencies to investigate and prosecute these crimes, and the increasing of cooperation with international partners to share information and best practices (Rijken, 2011).

Money laundering in the UAE plays a key role in both the facilitation of human trafficking and prostitution as well as the continuation of these illegal activities. Laundering money supports the expansion of illegal activities by supplying criminals with the finances and cover they need to continue their operations. This weakens the nation's attempts to resist these illegal activities. The United Arab Emirates (UAE) needs to establish comprehensive anti-money laundering (AML) measures, reinforce its legal and regulatory frameworks, and create more international collaboration in order to successfully handle this issue.

2.   Impact on UAE Society

The involvement of mafia organizations in human trafficking and prostitution has several negative consequences for the UAE society, including:

a. Undermining Social Stability: The presence of organized crime groups involved in human trafficking and prostitution can undermine social stability, contributing to crime and violence in the nation (Shelley, 2014).

Laundering money, which is the practice of disguising the sources of monies that have been unlawfully obtained, has a substantial influence on the social stability of the United Arab Emirates (UAE) since it enables and maintains human trafficking. According to Shelley (2014), human trafficking, also known as the recruitment, transportation, and exploitation of persons for the purpose of forced labor or commercial sex, is a significant violation of human rights and erodes the social fabric of the UAE.

Because it gives criminal organizations a way to conceal the profits they make from human trafficking, money laundering enables these organizations to carry on their activities with a certain degree of freedom from legal repercussions.

Criminals are able to bribe public authorities, infiltrate legitimate enterprises, and elude law enforcement because of the enormous quantities of money generated through trafficking (FATF, 2018). This corruption undermines the UAE's social stability by eroding public faith in institutions and contributing to an atmosphere of lawlessness.

b. Exploitation of Vulnerable Populations: The victims of human trafficking and prostitution, often drawn from economically disadvantaged backgrounds, suffer significant physical, psychological, and emotional harm as a result of their exploitation (United Nations, 2018).

Victims of human trafficking in the United Arab Emirates frequently suffer from physical, psychological, and emotional stress, which can have long-term repercussions for the victims' well-being as well as their ability to integrate into society. According to the United States Department of State's estimates for 2020, a significant number of victims are non-citizens who were tricked into traveling to the United Arab Emirates (UAE) on false pretenses and who were then exploited in scenarios such as forced labor, domestic slavery, or commercial sex.

The stigmatization and exclusion of these individuals exacerbate the social divisions and tensions that already exist within the UAE, further compromising the country's capacity to maintain social cohesion.

The pervasive use of money laundering as a tool to promote human trafficking in the UAE has wider-reaching ramifications for both the stability of the region and the world as a whole. According to Shelley (2014), the United Arab Emirates runs the risk of becoming a hub for transnational organized crime as criminal networks become more sophisticated and integrated. This has the potential to destabilize surrounding nations and fuel conflicts in the area.

It is vital to implement a comprehensive approach that encompasses legal, regulatory, and social interventions in order to address the interconnected problems of money laundering and people trafficking in the UAE. This approach should incorporate all three types of interventions. It is possible for authorities to identify and disrupt the financial flows that allow human trafficking networks to function by strengthening anti-money laundering measures, enhancing financial surveillance, and investing in the capacity of financial intelligence units to detect and analyze suspicious transactions (FATF, 2018). These are all things that can be accomplished by strengthening anti-money laundering measures.

Communities can be empowered to play a more proactive role in the fight against these crimes if they are made more aware of the warning signs of human trafficking and encouraged to report suspicious activity. According to the United States Department of State's 2020 report, providing victims with support services such as safe shelters, counseling, legal assistance, and vocational training can assist them in recovering from their experiences and reintegrating into society, thereby mitigating the negative impact that human trafficking has on the social stability of a community.

Addressing the relationship between money laundering and human trafficking is essential for maintaining social stability in the UAE. This link has been established through extensive investigation. The United Arab Emirates (UAE) has the potential to make strides toward a society that is both safer and more just if it adopts a holistic strategy that takes aim at both the financial facilitators of these crimes and their human repercussions.

3. Countermeasures

The UAE has put in place a number of countermeasures in response to the growing threat that mafia organizations pose and their involvement in money laundering, financial crimes, human trafficking, and prostitution, including:

a. Strengthening Legal Frameworks: The UAE has enacted stricter anti-money laundering and human trafficking laws, imposing severe penalties for these crimes and providing greater protections for victims (FATF, 2020; UAE Federal Law No. 51, 2006).

The United Arab Emirates (UAE) has been grappling with the issue of illicit financial flows and their associated risks, which have been facilitated in part by the country's inadequate legal frameworks. Despite some progress in recent years, the UAE's legal and regulatory environment remains vulnerable to exploitation by organized crime and corruption (Carnegie Endowment for International Peace, 2020).

One of the main factors contributing to the UAE's vulnerability to illicit financial flows is the lack of a comprehensive and robust legal framework to address money laundering, terrorist financing, and other financial crimes. While the UAE has introduced some anti-money laundering (AML) and counter-terrorism financing (CTF) regulations, these measures have not been consistently enforced, leaving ample room for criminal actors to exploit the system (Carnegie Endowment for International Peace, 2020). This lack of enforcement is exacerbated by weak oversight and supervision by the country's regulatory authorities, as well as the existence of numerous free trade zones, each with their own set of rules and regulations, which further complicates enforcement efforts (Hutchings & Guala, 2017).

Another contributing factor to the UAE's vulnerability is its strict secrecy laws, which hinder transparency and information sharing, both domestically and internationally. These laws have made it difficult for international partners and law enforcement agencies to access crucial information needed for investigations and prosecutions, thereby limiting the effectiveness of efforts to combat financial crime (Carnegie Endowment for International Peace, 2020).

In addition, the UAE's legal system has been criticized for its lack of independence and impartiality, with concerns raised about the influence of powerful individuals and interests on the judiciary. This lack of independence has undermined efforts to hold powerful actors accountable and has contributed to a culture of impunity for financial crimes (Carnegie Endowment for International Peace, 2020).

To address these shortcomings and strengthen its legal framework, the UAE must undertake several key reforms. Firstly, it needs to enhance its AML/CTF regulations and ensure their consistent enforcement across all sectors and jurisdictions within the country. This will require investing in capacity building for regulatory authorities and law enforcement agencies, as well as fostering a culture of transparency and accountability (Hutchings & Guala, 2017).

Secondly, the UAE must address the issue of secrecy laws and improve information sharing, both domestically and with international partners, to facilitate the investigation and prosecution of financial crimes. This will involve revising existing secrecy laws and promoting greater transparency in the financial sector (Carnegie Endowment for International Peace, 2020).

Lastly, the UAE must strengthen the independence and impartiality of its judiciary to ensure that all actors, regardless of their power and influence, can be held accountable for financial crimes. This will require comprehensive judicial reform and a commitment to upholding the rule of law.

b. Enhancing Law Enforcement Capacity: The UAE has increased its law enforcement capacity to combat organized crime, investing in training, equipment, and intelligence-sharing initiatives to enhance the effectiveness of its efforts (UNODC, 2016).

The United Arab Emirates (UAE) has made some progress in enhancing its law enforcement capacity to combat organized crime and corruption. However, recent reports suggest that these efforts have not yet met international standards, allowing kleptocrats and criminal networks to continue thriving within the country (Carnegie Endowment for International Peace, 2020).

One major challenge facing the UAE's law enforcement agencies is their lack of capacity to effectively investigate and prosecute complex financial crimes, particularly those involving high-level officials and politically connected individuals (Carnegie Endowment for International Peace, 2020). This deficiency stems from a lack of expertise, resources, and political will to pursue such cases, which often involve powerful actors with significant influence over the country's political and economic landscape (Hutchings & Guala, 2017).

Furthermore, the UAE's legal framework has been criticized for its opacity and inconsistencies, which have complicated efforts to combat organized crime and corruption. For example, the country's numerous free trade zones, each with its own set of regulations and enforcement mechanisms, have created opportunities for criminals to exploit regulatory gaps and circumvent national and international controls (Hutchings & Guala, 2017). Additionally, the UAE's strict secrecy laws have hindered information sharing and cooperation with international partners, further undermining the effectiveness of its law enforcement efforts (Carnegie Endowment for International Peace, 2020).

Another area of concern is the UAE's weak and inconsistent implementation of its anti-money laundering (AML) and counter-terrorism financing (CTF) regulations. Despite the fact that the nation has made efforts to strengthen its AML/CTF framework, these initiatives have failed due to administrative challenges, insufficient enforcement, and a lack of political will to address the causes of organized crime and corruption (US Department of State, 2021).

Moreover, the UAE's law enforcement agencies have been criticized for their selective approach to tackling organized crime, with a particular focus on low-level offenders while neglecting high-profile cases involving powerful individuals and well-established criminal networks (Carnegie Endowment for International Peace, 2020). This selective approach has raised concerns about the impartiality and effectiveness of the UAE's law enforcement efforts, with critics arguing that the country's political and economic elite have largely been shielded from scrutiny and accountability (Hutchings & Guala, 2017).

In order to address these challenges and bring its law enforcement capacity in line with international standards, the UAE must undertake a comprehensive reform of its legal and regulatory framework, invest in building the capacity of its law enforcement agencies, and demonstrate a genuine commitment to tackling organized crime and corruption at all levels. This will require not only addressing the technical and capacity-related challenges facing the country's law enforcement agencies but also fostering a culture of transparency, accountability, and political will to confront the powerful actors involved in organized crime and corruption.

c. International Cooperation: The UAE has engaged in international cooperation with other countries and regional organizations, such as Europol and Interpol, to share information, disrupt organized crime networks, and apprehend key individuals involved in these activities (Europol, 2018).

Recent assessments imply that international collaboration on dismantling criminal networks has been falling short (Carnegie Endowment for International Peace, 2020). This is despite the efforts of the United Arab Emirates (UAE) to combat organized crime. While the United Arab Emirates (UAE) has made some headway in improving its framework for anti-money laundering (AML) and countering the financing of terrorism (CTF), the country still faces challenges in effectively implementing these measures and working with international partners to address the complicated problem of organized crime (US Department of State, 2021).

According to the Carnegie Endowment for International Peace (2020), one of the primary sources of worry is the role that Dubai plays in enabling global illegal cash flows and corruption. Because of its fast economic development, strategic position, and thriving financial sector, the emirate has attracted both lawful firms and criminal groups that are looking to take advantage of these advantages for their own nefarious objectives. Because of this, Dubai has become a center for money laundering, corruption, and other financial crimes, which undermines the United Arab Emirates' attempts to protect the country's financial integrity and fight organized crime (Carnegie Endowment for International Peace, 2020).

According to Hutchings and Guala (2017), a lack of effective international collaboration and information sharing between the UAE and its partners is one of the most significant hurdles that must be overcome in order to solve these concerns. Bureaucratic roadblocks, lax enforcement, and limited capacity have hindered these efforts (US Department of State, 2021). Although the UAE has taken steps to enhance its collaboration with foreign counterparts, such as the establishment of the Financial Intelligence Unit (FIU) and the adoption of international AML/CTF standards, these efforts have not been successful (US Department of State, 2021).

According to research published by the Carnegie Endowment for International Peace in 2020, the legal structure of the United Arab Emirates is both convoluted and murky, which has further hindered attempts to combat organized crime and illegal money flows. According to Hutchings and Guala (2017), the multiple free trade zones spread across the United States have provided opportunities for criminals to exploit regulatory gaps and evade national and international authorities. Each of these free trade zones has its own distinct collection of rules and procedures for law enforcement.

The unwillingness of the UAE to address politically sensitive issues, such as the presence of high-profile criminals and the involvement of powerful individuals in illicit activities, is another factor that contributes to the failure of international cooperation (Carnegie Endowment for International Peace, 2020). This has resulted in a lack of political will and commitment to successfully combat organized crime and the hazards connected with it, which has undermined the efficacy of efforts to cooperate internationally (Hutchings & Guala, 2017).

The presence of mafia organizations in the UAE poses significant challenges for the nation's society, economy, and security. However, by implementing effective countermeasures and engaging in international cooperation, the UAE can continue to combat the activities of these groups and minimize their impact on the nation's ongoing growth and development.

While the UAE has made progress in improving its AML/CTF framework and enhancing international cooperation, significant challenges remain in effectively addressing organized crime and illicit financial flows. To overcome these challenges, the UAE must strengthen its legal and regulatory framework, enhance enforcement capacity, and demonstrate greater political will to tackle the complex and multifaceted issue of organized crime. Only through sustained efforts and a genuine commitment to international cooperation can the UAE effectively combat criminal networks and safeguard its stability, prosperity, and international reputation.

THE NEXUS BETWEEN DRUG CARTELS AND THE MAFIA

A. Mutual Interests and Collaboration

1. Overview

In recent years, it has become more feasible for organized criminal groups such as drug cartels and mafia organizations to find common ground and collaborate with one another. As a direct result of this, they have begun working together in order to widen the scope of their illicit operations and take advantage of lucrative markets all over the world (Bagley, 2014). This connection is being pushed by the shared goals of the two organizations, which are to increase profits, avoid law enforcement, and maintain a competitive advantage in the underworld on a global scale (Glenny, 2008).

2. Areas of Collaboration

Drug cartels and mafia organizations collaborate in various criminal activities, including:

a. Drug Trafficking: Drug cartels rely on mafia organizations to facilitate the transportation, distribution, and sale of narcotics in consumer markets, particularly in Europe and North America (Shelley, 2014). In return, mafia groups profit from the drug trade, generating significant revenues that can be used to finance other criminal activities (Bagley, 2014).

The growing nexus between drug trafficking and Middle Eastern terrorist groups is a matter of increasing concern for global security. This connection poses significant challenges to regional stability, as terrorist organizations are turning to drug trafficking to finance their operations (Washington Institute, 2008).

Middle Eastern terrorist groups, such as Hezbollah, have established connections with drug cartels and mafia organizations, exploiting the drug trade to generate revenue for their activities. These groups facilitate the smuggling of drugs, including cocaine, heroin, and synthetic narcotics, through routes that traverse the Middle East and North Africa, ultimately reaching consumer markets in Europe, Asia, and the United States (Washington Institute, 2008).

The increasing involvement of terrorist organizations in drug trafficking can be attributed to several factors. Firstly, the drug trade is a highly lucrative business, offering substantial profits that can be used to fund terrorist activities. Secondly, the global nature of drug trafficking networks provides terrorist groups with the opportunity to forge alliances with other criminal organizations, further expanding their reach and capabilities (Washington Institute, 2008).

The United Arab Emirates (UAE), with its strategic location and well-developed infrastructure, has emerged as a hub for drug trafficking and a transit point for narcotics destined for other regions. This has attracted the attention of Middle Eastern terrorist groups, which seek to exploit the UAE's logistical advantages for their drug smuggling operations (Hutchings & Guala, 2017).

The close relationship between drug trafficking and terrorism has significant implications for the security and stability of the Middle East as well as the global community. The involvement of terrorist groups in the drug trade not only provides them with financial resources but also allows them to establish networks and partnerships that can facilitate the planning and execution of terrorist attacks (Washington Institute, 2008).

To effectively combat the growing nexus between drug trafficking and Middle Eastern terrorist groups, a comprehensive and coordinated approach is required. This includes enhancing intelligence sharing and cooperation among countries in the region, as well as with international partners, to better understand and disrupt the operations of these criminal networks (Washington Institute, 2008).

Moreover, efforts should be made to strengthen the capacity of law enforcement agencies and regulatory authorities in the region, empowering them to identify, investigate, and dismantle drug trafficking networks linked to terrorist organizations. This requires the implementation of robust legal and regulatory frameworks as well as the allocation of resources for training and capacity building (Hutchings & Guala, 2017).

Ultimately, addressing the growing nexus between drug trafficking and Middle Eastern terrorist groups requires a sustained and collaborative effort from the international community. By working together to disrupt the operations of these criminal networks, countries can help enhance regional stability and promote global security.

Drug cartels and mafia organizations collaborate in drug trafficking within the UAE through various means, such as:

Transit Hub: The UAE's strategic location between drug-producing regions like Afghanistan and consumer markets in Europe, Africa, and Asia makes it an attractive transit hub for narcotics. Drug cartels and mafia organizations collaborate by using the UAE's extensive transportation infrastructure, including its ports, airports, and free trade zones, to facilitate the movement of drugs (UNODC, 2016).

Local Criminal Networks: Mafia groups with an established presence in the UAE, such as the Russian mob and Israeli organized crime, can provide drug cartels with access to local criminal networks that can help in the distribution and sale of narcotics within the UAE and the broader region (Katz & Choate, 2017).

Corruption: To facilitate their drug trafficking operations, cartels and mafia organizations might seek to corrupt local officials in the UAE. By offering bribes or other incentives, they can secure the cooperation of customs officers, law enforcement agents, or other public officials who can turn a blind eye to their activities (Shelley, 2014).

Mafia organizations have increasingly targeted the United Arab Emirates (UAE) as a hub for their illicit activities, including attempts to corrupt local officials. The Organized Crime and Corruption Reporting Project (OCCRP) has revealed how officials, sanctioned politicians, and criminals have injected money into Dubai's real estate market through data leak investigations (OCCRP, 2021).

The data leak, which comprised more than 54,000 property and residency records, revealed that numerous high-ranking officials and individuals with criminal ties have invested in Dubai's real estate sector. These individuals have used the UAE's lax regulations, secretive financial system, and weak anti-money laundering (AML) measures to launder their illicit proceeds and evade international sanctions (OCCRP, 2021).

Mafia organizations have sought to exploit these vulnerabilities in the UAE's regulatory framework by establishing connections with local officials. Corrupt officials can facilitate the entry of illicit funds into the country, enabling criminal networks to invest in various sectors, including real estate, without raising suspicion (Carnegie Endowment, 2020).

The corruption of local officials in the UAE has significant consequences for the country's financial integrity and reputation as a global financial center. It undermines the effectiveness of AML measures as well as efforts to combat organized crime and terrorism financing (Carnegie Endowment, 2020).

Furthermore, the involvement of local officials in facilitating money laundering activities can erode public trust in government institutions and contribute to the spread of corruption throughout the country. This has the potential to destabilize the UAE's political and social systems, ultimately undermining its economic growth and development (OCCRP, 2021).

b. Money Laundering: Both drug cartels and mafia organizations engage in money laundering activities, often working together to launder the proceeds of their criminal enterprises through the global financial system (FATF, 2020). This collaboration allows them to legitimize their illicit profits, invest in legitimate businesses, and evade detection by law enforcement authorities (Galeotti, 2017).

To finance their drug trafficking operations, cartels and mafia organizations often engage in money laundering within the UAE's financial system. For instance, they might use the UAE's extensive network of hawala brokers, an informal money transfer system, to transfer funds across borders without detection (FATF, 2020).

c. Shell Companies and Trade-Based Money Laundering: Drug cartels and mafia groups can exploit the UAE's business-friendly environment to set up shell companies or engage in trade-based money laundering. By over- or under-invoicing, the value of goods in international trade transactions, these criminal networks can move illicit proceeds generated from drug trafficking (FATF, 2020).

d. Arms Trafficking: Drug cartels and mafia organizations also collaborate in the trafficking of weapons, with cartels supplying mafia groups with firearms and other weapons in exchange for their logistical support and protection (Shelley, 2014). These arms trades not only fuels violence and instability in the affected regions but also strengthens the criminal networks involved, making them more formidable adversaries for law enforcement agencies (Bagley, 2014).

Money laundering and arms trafficking are closely linked, as both involve the movement of illicit funds and goods. In the UAE, money laundering has been associated with arms trafficking, posing a threat to regional stability and the integrity of the country's financial system.

The UAE's free trade zones (FTZs) offer significant tax and regulatory advantages to businesses operating within their boundaries. However, these benefits have also attracted criminal networks engaged in money laundering and arms trafficking (Hutchings & Guala, 2017). Criminal organizations may use shell companies or front businesses in FTZs to launder money and facilitate the illicit trade in arms (FATF, 2020).

Some financial institutions in the UAE have been accused of facilitating transactions related to arms trafficking. In 2011, HSBC was found to have facilitated transactions for an arms dealer who had supplied weapons to Iran, in violation of international sanctions

(Reuters, 2012). This case highlighted the risk of money laundering and arms trafficking through the UAE's financial system.

Arms traffickers and other criminal organizations may use informal money transfer systems, such as hawala, to finance their operations in the UAE. These systems operate outside the formal financial sector, making it difficult for authorities to monitor and regulate transactions related to arms trafficking (FATF, 2020).

The UAE's proximity to conflict zones in the Middle East and North Africa has increased the risk of arms trafficking and money laundering in the country. As a major arms exporter, the UAE has been accused of supplying weapons to parties involved in regional conflicts, such as the war in Yemen (Human Rights Watch, 2019). These arms transfers can be facilitated through money laundering schemes that obscure the true origin and destination of the funds and weapons.

In some cases, government officials or other public figures in the UAE may be implicated in money laundering and arms trafficking schemes. This corruption can undermine the government's efforts to combat these crimes and erode public trust in the country's institutions (Shelley, 2014).

Viktor Bout's Role in UAE Arms Trafficking

Viktor Bout, a notorious international arms dealer dubbed the "Merchant of Death," played a significant role in facilitating arms trafficking in the United Arab Emirates (UAE) during his criminal career. Born in the Soviet Union, Bout gained infamy for his extensive network of illicit arms trading that spanned continents, fueled conflicts, and contributed to the destabilization of numerous regions (Farah & Braun, 2007). This section examines Bout's involvement in arms trafficking in the UAE and its implications for the nation's security and reputation.

During the late 1990s and early 2000s, the UAE emerged as a hub for global arms trafficking, thanks in part to Bout's extensive operations in the country (Farah & Braun, 2007). Dubai, with its strategic location, lax regulations, and thriving business environment, provided an ideal base for Bout to establish front companies that facilitated his illegal arms trade. These companies served as a cover for his activities, allowing him to transport weapons to conflict zones and embargoed nations with minimal scrutiny (Schmidt, 2012).

Bout's presence in the UAE was not entirely clandestine, as he maintained a high-profile lifestyle, socializing with influential figures and even attending high-profile events, such as air shows, to promote his aviation business (Farah & Braun, 2007). His ability to operate so brazenly in the UAE is indicative of the challenges the country faced in combating organized crime and enforcing arms trafficking regulations during this period.

The implications of Bout's operations in the UAE were far-reaching, as his arms trafficking activities contributed to regional instability and conflict. For example, Bout's network was implicated in supplying weapons to various factions in Afghanistan, including the Taliban and Al-Qaeda, thus fueling the insurgency against U.S. and NATO forces in the country (Chivers, 2008). Additionally, Bout was known to have trafficked arms to African warlords, further exacerbating ongoing civil wars and humanitarian crises on the continent (Farah & Braun, 2007).

Bout's activities also had significant consequences for the UAE's reputation and standing in the international community. As his operations became more widely known, the UAE faced increased scrutiny and criticism for its perceived failure to adequately combat arms trafficking within its borders (Schmidt, 2012). This not only harmed the nation's image but also strained relations with its allies, particularly the United States, which ultimately led to Bout's arrest in a joint U.S.-Thai sting operation in 2008 (Kaplan, 2008).

In conclusion, Viktor Bout's involvement in arms trafficking in the UAE underscores the challenges the country faces in addressing the activities of organized crime networks operating within its borders. His operations in the UAE had significant consequences, both domestically and internationally, as they fueled conflicts, destabilized regions, and tarnished the nation's reputation. Addressing the issue of arms trafficking and its connection to organized crime remains a critical priority for the UAE and the broader international community in order to maintain global security and stability.

B. The Global Impact of Their Alliance

1. Destabilizing Influence

The nexus between drug cartels and mafia organizations has significant implications for global security and stability, as their collaboration fuels crime, violence, and corruption in affected countries (Glenny, 2008). This destabilizing influence can undermine governance, weaken the rule of law, and erode public confidence in government institutions, creating a fertile environment for the further expansion of their criminal activities (Shelley, 2014).

One of the key factors contributing to this destabilizing influence is the vast number of resources and power that drug cartels and mafia organizations command. These criminal networks generate substantial profits from their illicit activities, which can be used to corrupt public officials, infiltrate law enforcement agencies, and fund violence against rivals and adversaries (UNODC, 2016). This corruption and violence can lead to a breakdown in social order as communities are terrorized and public institutions lose their legitimacy in the eyes of citizens (Cockayne & Lupel, 2011).

Moreover, the collusion between drug cartels and mafia organizations can exacerbate existing social and economic inequalities. These criminal networks often exploit vulnerable populations, such as marginalized communities, migrants, and disadvantaged youth, as a source of recruits, suppliers, and consumers for their illegal activities (Carpenter, 2016). As a result, these communities can become trapped in cycles of poverty, violence, and criminality, further undermining social cohesion and sustainable development (UNODC, 2016).

The global nature of these criminal networks also complicates efforts to combat their destabilizing influence. Drug cartels and mafia organizations often operate across national borders, taking advantage of weak governance, porous borders, and the increasing interconnectedness of the global economy to expand their reach and evade law enforcement (Europol, 2020). This transnational dimension requires a coordinated international response to effectively disrupt and dismantle these networks (FATF, 2020).

Dubai has become a focal point for concerns related to the circumvention of international sanctions against Russia (Burgis & Aglionby, 2023). As a global financial and trading hub, the UAE has the potential to act as a facilitator for evading sanctions, raising questions about its commitment to upholding international law and contributing to global security and stability.

The UAE has maintained strong trade and economic ties with Russia, even in the face of mounting international pressure due to Russia's actions in various conflicts (Burgis & Aglionby, 2023). As a result, Dubai has emerged as a preferred destination for Russian businesses and individuals seeking to avoid the impact of sanctions imposed by the United States, the European Union, and other countries.

There have been reports of Russian companies and individuals using Dubai's financial infrastructure and free trade zones to conduct transactions and transfer assets in a way that evades detection by international regulators (Burgis & Aglionby, 2023). Dubai's advanced financial services sector, coupled with its relatively lax regulatory environment, has made it an attractive destination for those seeking to bypass sanctions.

Moreover, Dubai's property market has become a popular destination for Russian investors seeking to safeguard their wealth and avoid scrutiny from international regulators (Burgis & Aglionby, 2023). The UAE's property registration system allows for a high degree of anonymity, making it easier for individuals and entities to hide their ownership of assets and evade the reach of sanctions.

The UAE's role in facilitating the circumvention of international sanctions against Russia raises concerns about its commitment to global security and stability. This situation undermines international efforts to hold Russia accountable for its actions and weakens the effectiveness of sanctions as a foreign policy tool (Europol, 2020). It also calls into question the UAE's willingness to cooperate with other countries in addressing transnational threats, such as organized crime and terrorism.

To address these concerns, the UAE must take concrete steps to strengthen its regulatory framework and enforcement mechanisms related to sanctions compliance. This includes increasing transparency in its financial and property sectors as well as improving cooperation with international partners to share information and best practices for combating sanctions evasion (FATF, 2020).

Additionally, the UAE should demonstrate its commitment to upholding international law and norms by aligning its policies and actions with global efforts to address the Russian threat. This may involve reassessing its economic ties with Russia and taking a more assertive stance in support of the implementation of sanctions.

Dubai's role in facilitating the circumvention of international sanctions against Russia highlights the need for the UAE to strengthen its regulatory framework and enforcement mechanisms related to sanctions compliance. By taking these steps, the UAE can demonstrate its commitment to upholding international law and contributing to global security and stability. Furthermore, addressing these issues will also help the UAE combat other transnational threats, such as organized crime and terrorism, more effectively.

To address the destabilizing influence of drug cartels and mafia organizations, governments and international organizations must work together to strengthen governance, enhance the rule of law, and promote social and economic development in affected countries. This includes implementing comprehensive anti-corruption measures, bolstering law enforcement capacity, and promoting economic opportunities for vulnerable populations to reduce their susceptibility to criminal exploitation (UNODC, 2016).

Furthermore, international cooperation and information sharing are essential for disrupting the global networks that enable the collaboration between drug cartels and mafia organizations. By working together and sharing resources, intelligence, and best practices, countries can enhance their ability to combat these complex and evolving threats (FATF, 2020).

The destabilizing influence of drug cartels and mafia organizations poses a significant threat to global security and stability. Addressing this challenge requires a multifaceted and collaborative approach focused on strengthening governance, promoting social and economic development, and enhancing international cooperation.

2. Economic Consequences

The alliance between drug cartels and mafia organizations has far-reaching negative economic consequences, as their illicit activities distort markets, undermine economic growth, and divert resources away from more productive sectors of the economy (Bagley, 2014). Additionally, their money laundering activities can compromise the integrity of the global financial system, exposing affected countries to reputational risks and potential sanctions from international organizations (FATF, 2020).

One of the most significant economic consequences of this alliance is the distortion of markets due to the massive influx of illicit funds. Drug cartels and mafia organizations generate substantial revenues through their criminal activities, which can lead to inflated asset prices, particularly in real estate and other high-value sectors (Passas, 2005). This distortion can create economic imbalances and contribute to the formation of speculative bubbles, which can have severe repercussions for financial stability and overall economic growth (Bagley, 2014).

Furthermore, the alliance between drug cartels and mafia organizations can lead to significant resource misallocation. As illicit funds are invested in unproductive or even harmful activities, such as arms trafficking, human smuggling, and environmental crimes, resources are diverted away from more productive sectors, such as education, healthcare, and infrastructure (UNODC, 2016). This misallocation can hinder economic development and exacerbate social and economic disparities, particularly in countries with high levels of organized crime (Shelley, 2014).

Money laundering is another critical economic consequence of the alliance between drug cartels and mafia organizations. As these criminal networks seek to conceal the origin and ownership of their illicit proceeds, they often engage in complex money laundering schemes that can penetrate and corrupt the global financial system (FATF, 2020). These activities can erode the integrity of financial institutions, compromise the effectiveness of anti-money laundering (AML) and counter-terrorist financing (CTF) measures, and expose affected countries to reputational risks, which can lead to reduced foreign investment, capital flight, and potential sanctions from international organizations (IMF, 2017).

To mitigate the economic consequences of the alliance between drug cartels and mafia organizations, governments and international organizations must implement robust AML/CTF measures, strengthen regulatory frameworks, and promote transparency and accountability in the financial sector (FATF, 2020). Additionally, they should invest in capacity-building and technical assistance to help affected countries identify and dismantle the criminal networks responsible for these activities and redirect resources towards more productive and sustainable uses (UNODC, 2016).

The alliance between drug cartels and mafia organizations has significant negative economic consequences for countries and the global financial system. Addressing these challenges requires a comprehensive and coordinated approach, including the implementation of robust AML/CTF measures, capacity building, and international cooperation.

C. The Dark Web and Cybercrime

1.   Exploiting the Dark Web

Drug cartels and mafia organizations have increasingly turned to the dark web to facilitate their criminal activities, exploiting the anonymity and encryption technologies offered by this hidden corner of the internet to evade law enforcement detection (Chertoff & Simon, 2015). The dark web enables these groups to engage in a range of illicit activities, including drug trafficking, arms smuggling, human trafficking, and the sale of counterfeit goods, with minimal risk of exposure (Europol, 2018).

The dark web's unique features, such as the use of the Tor network for anonymous browsing and the proliferation of cryptocurrencies for secure and untraceable transactions, have made it an attractive platform for criminal enterprises (Afilipoaie & Shortis, 2019). These technologies allow drug cartels and mafia organizations to communicate, coordinate, and conduct business without the risk of interception by law enforcement agencies, making it more challenging to disrupt their operations and bring them to justice (Chertoff & Simon, 2015).

Moreover, the dark web has facilitated the globalization of organized crime by providing a virtual marketplace for illicit goods and services (Europol, 2018). Through darknet marketplaces, drug cartels and mafia organizations can connect with suppliers, distributors, and customers from around the world, expanding their reach and increasing their profits (Afilipoaie & Shortis, 2019). This global dimension further complicates efforts to combat organized crime, as it requires unprecedented levels of international cooperation and coordination (Europol, 2020).

The dark web has also contributed to the diversification of organized crime activities as drug cartels and mafia organizations increasingly venture into new and emerging criminal markets, such as cybercrime and environmental crime (Europol, 2018). This diversification not only generates additional revenue streams for these criminal networks but also exposes them to new opportunities for collaboration with other criminal groups, potentially exacerbating the threat they pose to global security and stability (Chertoff & Simon, 2015).

To counter the exploitation of the dark web by drug cartels and mafia organizations, law enforcement agencies and policymakers must develop innovative strategies and invest in cutting-edge technologies to infiltrate and disrupt these hidden criminal networks (Europol,

2020). This includes enhancing cyber capabilities, promoting information sharing and collaboration among national and international agencies, and developing legislative frameworks that enable the effective prosecution of dark web-enabled crimes (Afilipoaie & Shortis, 2019).

Additionally, efforts must be made to raise public awareness of the risks associated with the dark web and the role it plays in facilitating organized crime (Chertoff & Simon, 2015). By promoting a better understanding of the dark web's dangers and encouraging responsible online behavior, policymakers and law enforcement agencies can help reduce the demand for illicit goods and services, thereby undermining the profitability of drug cartels and mafia organizations operating on the dark web (Europol, 2018).

The exploitation of the dark web by drug cartels and mafia organizations represents a significant challenge for global security and stability. Addressing this challenge requires a multifaceted approach, including technological advancements, enhanced international cooperation, and public awareness campaigns.

2. Cybercrime

The nexus between drug cartels and mafia organizations extends to the realm of cybercrime, as both groups increasingly rely on sophisticated technology and cyber capabilities to advance their criminal enterprises (Chertoff & Simon, 2015). This may include the use of malware, ransomware, and other cyber tools to target financial institutions, extort businesses, and steal sensitive data, generating significant profits for these criminal networks (Europol, 2018).

The convergence of organized crime and cybercrime presents a formidable challenge for law enforcement agencies and policymakers, as it combines the resources, expertise, and global reach of drug cartels and mafia organizations with the rapidly evolving and often elusive nature of cyber threats (Carrapico & Farrand, 2017). This potent combination enables these criminal networks to conduct large-scale, high-impact attacks that can have far-reaching consequences for individuals, businesses, and governments (Europol, 2018).

One notable example of this convergence is the increasing use of ransomware attacks by drug cartels and mafia organizations. These attacks involve encrypting the victim's data and demanding a ransom, usually in the form of cryptocurrency, for the decryption key (Chertoff & Simon, 2015). Ransomware attacks have become a lucrative source of income for criminal networks, with victims often paying significant sums to regain access to their data and systems (Europol, 2018).

Furthermore, drug cartels and mafia organizations have demonstrated a growing interest in targeting critical infrastructure, such as energy grids, transportation systems, and healthcare facilities, through cyberattacks (Carrapico & Farrand, 2017). These attacks can cause significant disruption and economic damage and, in some cases, even pose a threat to public safety and national security (Europol, 2018).

To effectively counter the growing nexus between drug cartels, mafia organizations, and cybercrime, law enforcement agencies must adapt their strategies and invest in new technologies and capabilities (Europol, 2020). This includes enhancing cyber forensics, developing advanced analytics and machine learning tools to identify and track criminal networks, and fostering greater collaboration between cyber experts and traditional organized crime investigators (Carrapico & Farrand, 2017).

In addition, international cooperation and information sharing are essential for combating the global nature of this threat. By working together and sharing resources, intelligence, and best practices, countries can enhance their ability to detect, disrupt, and dismantle the criminal networks responsible for these increasingly sophisticated cyberattacks (Europol, 2020).

Furthermore, public-private partnerships can play a vital role in addressing the convergence of organized crime and cybercrime. By collaborating with industry stakeholders and leveraging their expertise, law enforcement agencies can gain valuable insights into emerging trends, vulnerabilities, and potential solutions, enhancing their overall effectiveness in combating this evolving threat (Carrapico & Farrand, 2017).

The growing nexus between drug cartels, mafia organizations, and cybercrime poses significant challenges for global security and stability. Addressing this threat requires a multifaceted approach, including the development of new technologies and capabilities, enhanced international cooperation, and the establishment of public-private partnerships.

3.   Countermeasures

To combat the growing threat posed by the nexus between drug cartels and mafia organizations, as well as their exploitation of the dark web and involvement in cybercrime, several countermeasures can be employed:

a. Enhancing Law Enforcement Cooperation: International cooperation between law enforcement agencies is essential to disrupt the activities of drug cartels and mafia organizations, particularly in the realm of cybercrime and dark web investigations (Europol, 2018). This may involve intelligence sharing, joint operations, and the development of specialized task forces to target these criminal networks (UNODC, 2016).

To address the growing collaboration between drug cartels and mafia organizations in the UAE, the country must take several steps. First, it must strengthen its legal and regulatory frameworks to combat money laundering and other financial crimes, ensuring consistent enforcement across all sectors and jurisdictions (Carnegie Endowment for International Peace, 2020). Second, the UAE should invest in capacity building for its law enforcement agencies and regulatory authorities, empowering them to identify and dismantle these criminal networks more effectively (Hutchings & Guala, 2017).

Finally, the UAE must work closely with international partners and organizations to share intelligence, enhance cooperation, and develop coordinated strategies to disrupt the operations of drug cartels and mafia groups.

b. Strengthening Legal Frameworks: Governments must continue to strengthen their legal frameworks to address the evolving nature of the threat posed by drug cartels and mafia organizations, including updating laws and regulations related to cybercrime, money laundering, and organized crime (FATF, 2020).

To address the issue of mafia organizations seeking to corrupt local officials in the UAE, several measures need to be implemented. Firstly, the UAE must strengthen its AML and counter-terrorism financing (CTF) frameworks by adopting international best practices and enhancing the capacity of its regulatory and law enforcement agencies. This includes increasing transparency in the real estate sector, implementing stricter due diligence requirements, and improving the exchange of information between domestic and international partners (Carnegie Endowment, 2020).

Secondly, the UAE should invest in efforts to prevent and combat corruption at all levels of government. This requires implementing robust anti-corruption policies, promoting transparency and accountability, and ensuring that public officials are held to the highest ethical standards (OCCRP, 2021).

Lastly, the international community should support the UAE in its efforts to combat corruption and organized crime by providing technical assistance, supporting capacity-building initiatives, and sharing best practices in AML and CTF efforts (Carnegie Endowment, 2020).

By implementing these measures, the UAE can enhance its resilience to the corrupting influence of mafia organizations and protect its financial integrity, economic stability, and global reputation.

c. Investing in Cybersecurity: Governments and businesses must prioritize investments in cybersecurity to protect their networks and critical infrastructure from the growing threat posed by drug cartels and mafia organizations (Chertoff & Simon, 2015). This includes investing in advanced technology, training, and personnel to detect and mitigate cyber threats and secure the digital landscape (Europol, 2018).

The United Arab Emirates (UAE) has emerged as a global financial hub and technological powerhouse. However, the country's rapid development has also attracted the attention of criminals, corrupt officials, and sanctioned politicians who exploit the UAE's digital infrastructure for their illicit activities (OCCRP, 2021). As a result, it is crucial for the UAE to invest in cybersecurity measures to protect its financial integrity and maintain its status as a leading global business destination.

The increasing reliance on digital technologies has created new opportunities for cybercriminals to target the UAE's financial institutions, businesses, and government agencies. Cyberattacks can result in the theft of sensitive data, disruption of critical services, and the potential compromise of national security (Alperovitch & Weidemann, 2017).

To mitigate these risks, the UAE must prioritize the development of robust cybersecurity strategies and invest in state-of-the-art technologies to detect, prevent, and respond to cyber threats. This includes strengthening the technical capacity of its cybersecurity agencies, investing in research and development, and fostering collaboration between the public and private sectors to ensure a comprehensive approach to cybersecurity (Alperovitch & Weidemann, 2017).

One of the primary challenges faced by the UAE in combating cybercrime is the lack of effective legislation and regulatory frameworks. To address this issue, the UAE should develop and implement comprehensive cybercrime laws that define and criminalize various forms of cyber offenses in line with international best practices (ITU, 2018). Furthermore, the UAE must enhance its legal and regulatory frameworks to facilitate cross-border cooperation in investigating and prosecuting cybercrimes, particularly when they involve money laundering, corruption, and other financial crimes (Carnegie Endowment, 2020).

Education and awareness-raising initiatives are also critical to building a cybersecurity culture in the UAE. The government should invest in cybersecurity education programs to equip individuals and organizations with the knowledge and skills needed to protect themselves against cyber threats (ITU, 2018). This includes promoting cybersecurity awareness among the general public as well as providing specialized training for professionals in sectors that are particularly vulnerable to cyberattacks, such as the financial and critical infrastructure sectors (Alperovitch & Weidemann, 2017).

In addition, the UAE should establish partnerships with international organizations, law enforcement agencies, and other countries to enhance its capacity to combat cybercrime. Collaborative efforts, such as sharing threat intelligence, best practices, and technical expertise, can significantly improve the effectiveness of the UAE's cybersecurity measures (Carnegie Endowment, 2020).

Strengthening public-private partnerships in cybersecurity is another crucial aspect for the UAE to consider. By fostering collaboration between government agencies and private sector organizations, the country can develop a more resilient cybersecurity infrastructure and facilitate information sharing on emerging threats and vulnerabilities (Alperovitch & Weidemann, 2017). These partnerships can also help establish industry-specific cybersecurity standards and best practices, which can contribute to the overall improvement of the UAE's cybersecurity posture.

Moreover, the UAE should focus on enhancing its cyber-threat intelligence capabilities. By actively monitoring, collecting, and analyzing information on potential cyber threats, the UAE can stay ahead of cybercriminals and anticipate their tactics, techniques, and procedures (TTPs) (Alperovitch & Weidemann, 2017). This intelligence-driven approach can enable a proactive response to emerging threats, reducing the likelihood of successful cyberattacks.

In the context of combating money laundering and illicit financial activities, the UAE should also invest in cutting-edge financial technologies (FinTech) and regulatory technologies (RegTech) to improve its anti-money laundering (AML) and countering the financing of terrorism (CFT) efforts (Carnegie Endowment, 2020). By leveraging artificial intelligence, machine learning, and big data analytics, these technologies can enhance the detection and reporting of suspicious transactions, streamline compliance processes, and facilitate more effective risk management.

Lastly, the UAE should consider developing a comprehensive national cybersecurity strategy that outlines its long-term vision and goals for enhancing its cybersecurity capabilities. This strategy should identify the key stakeholders, roles, and responsibilities in the country's cybersecurity ecosystem, as well as provide a roadmap for achieving its objectives (ITU, 2018). By establishing a clear strategic framework, the UAE can ensure a coordinated and effective response to the evolving cyber threat landscape and demonstrate its commitment to upholding international standards in cybersecurity.

d. Raising Public Awareness: Governments and civil society organizations should work together to raise public awareness about the dangers posed by the nexus between drug cartels and mafia organizations, as well as the risks associated with the dark web and cybercrime (Chertoff & Simon, 2015). Public education campaigns, community engagement initiatives, and partnerships with the private sector can help to foster a culture of cybersecurity and vigilance against these threats (Europol, 2018).

The nexus between drug cartels and mafia organizations poses a significant threat to the security and stability of the UAE, as well as to the well-being of its citizens. In order to effectively combat this issue, it is vital that the UAE government work to raise public awareness about the dangers posed by these criminal networks and their illicit activities. Public awareness campaigns can play a crucial role in fostering a culture of vigilance and enhancing the ability of individuals and communities to recognize and report suspicious activities (Europol, 2020).

One of the key aspects of raising public awareness is to educate the population about the various methods used by drug cartels and mafia organizations to smuggle and distribute narcotics, launder money, and engage in human trafficking. This can be done through public service announcements, awareness campaigns, and educational materials distributed to schools, universities, and community centers (U.S. Department of State, 2016). By providing citizens with a better understanding of these criminal activities, they can become more vigilant in identifying and reporting suspicious behavior.

In addition, the UAE should also engage in efforts to address the root causes of organized crime, such as poverty, unemployment, and social inequality. By providing at-risk communities with better access to education, employment opportunities, and social services, the government can help reduce the allure of joining criminal networks (United Nations Office on Drugs and Crime, 2010).

The UAE government should also collaborate with civil society organizations and community leaders to promote a culture of lawfulness and integrity. By fostering partnerships between government agencies, non-governmental organizations, and community-based organizations, the UAE can develop and implement targeted interventions to address the specific needs and vulnerabilities of different communities (United Nations Office on Drugs and Crime, 2010).

Furthermore, the UAE should strengthen its international cooperation and collaboration with other countries and organizations in the fight against organized crime. By participating in regional and global forums, sharing intelligence and best practices, and providing technical assistance and capacity-building support to other countries, the UAE can contribute to the global effort to combat the threats posed by drug cartels and mafia organizations (Europol, 2020).

Finally, it is important for the UAE to continuously evaluate the effectiveness of its public awareness campaigns and other efforts to combat organized crime. By conducting regular assessments and incorporating feedback from stakeholders, the government can ensure that its strategies remain relevant and responsive to the evolving threat landscape (U.S. Department of State, 2016).

In conclusion, the nexus between drug cartels and mafia organizations has emerged as a significant global threat, with their collaboration in various criminal activities posing challenges to security, stability, and economic development. The increasing involvement of these groups in the dark web and cybercrime further underscores the complexity and scale of the problem. By adopting a comprehensive and coordinated approach that emphasizes international cooperation, legal reform, investment in cybersecurity, and public awareness, governments and stakeholders can work together to counter the activities of these criminal networks and mitigate their impact on society.

THE UAE'S RESPONSE TO ORGANIZED CRIME

A. Law Enforcement Strategies and Challenges

1. Strengthening Legal Frameworks

The Over the years, the UAE has made concerted efforts to strengthen its legal framework in order to effectively combat organized crime, money laundering, and other illicit activities. The country has implemented a series of laws and regulations aimed at enhancing its capacity to prevent, investigate, and prosecute criminal activities while also fostering cooperation with international partners and organizations (FATF, 2020).

One of the key steps taken by the UAE government has been the enactment of the Anti-Money Laundering and Combating the Financing of Terrorism (AML/CFT) Law in 2018 (Federal Law No. 20 of 2018). This legislation provides a comprehensive framework for the prevention, investigation, and prosecution of money laundering and terrorist financing activities, as well as for the establishment of the Financial Intelligence Unit (FIU) and the Anti-Money Laundering and Suspicious Cases Unit (AMLSCU) (UAE Central Bank, 2018). The law also mandates the reporting of suspicious transactions by financial institutions, designated non-financial businesses and professions, and other obligated entities (FATF, 2020).

In addition to the AML/CFT Law, the UAE has implemented several other legal instruments aimed at combating organized crime, such as the Cyber Crimes Law (Federal Law No. 5 of 2012), which criminalizes various forms of cybercrime, including hacking, identity theft, and online fraud. The law also provides for the establishment of specialized units within the country's law enforcement agencies to investigate and prosecute cybercrimes (Gulf News, 2012).

The UAE has also adopted a series of laws and regulations aimed at combating human trafficking, such as Federal Law No. 51 of 2006 on Combating Human Trafficking Crimes. This legislation provides for severe penalties for human trafficking offenses and establishes a national committee responsible for coordinating efforts to combat trafficking (U.S. Department of State, 2020).

In an effort to foster international cooperation and enhance its capacity to combat transnational organized crime, the UAE has also ratified several international conventions, including the United Nations Convention against Transnational Organized Crime (UNTOC) and its protocols, as well as the United Nations Convention against Corruption (UNCAC) (United Nations Office on Drugs and Crime, 2019).

Moreover, the UAE has made significant efforts to improve its regulatory framework for financial institutions and designated non-financial businesses and professions. The Central Bank of the UAE has issued a series of regulations and guidelines aimed at enhancing the transparency and accountability of the financial sector, including the development of risk-based supervision and compliance frameworks (UAE Central Bank, 2020).

Despite these efforts, the UAE must continue to strengthen its legal frameworks and invest in capacity building for its law enforcement agencies, regulatory authorities, and judiciary in order to effectively combat organized crime and other illicit activities.

2. Enhancing Law Enforcement Capacity

The UAE has undertaken various initiatives to enhance its law enforcement capacity with the aim of effectively combating organized crime, money laundering, and other illicit activities. These efforts encompass training and capacity-building programs, the establishment of specialized units, and increased international cooperation (FATF, 2020).

One of the significant steps taken by the UAE has been the establishment of the Financial Intelligence Unit (FIU) and the Anti-Money Laundering and Suspicious Cases Unit (AMLSCU), as mandated by the Anti-Money Laundering and Combating the Financing of Terrorism (AML/CFT) Law (Federal Law No. 20 of 2018). These units are responsible for receiving, analyzing, and disseminating financial intelligence related to money laundering, terrorist financing, and other financial crimes (UAE Central Bank, 2018).

In addition, the UAE has established specialized units within its law enforcement agencies to combat various forms of organized crime, such as the Cyber Crimes Law (Federal Law No. 5 of 2012), which led to the creation of dedicated cybercrime units to investigate and prosecute cybercrimes (Gulf News, 2012).

Capacity-building and training programs have been essential aspects of the UAE's efforts to enhance its law enforcement capacity. The UAE has organized various training programs for its law enforcement officers, prosecutors, and judges, focusing on the investigation and prosecution of organized crime, money laundering, terrorist financing, and other related offenses (U.S. Department of State, 2020).

Furthermore, the UAE has been actively engaging in international cooperation to strengthen its law enforcement capacity. The country is a member of the Egmont Group of Financial Intelligence Units, which facilitates the exchange of financial intelligence among its members to combat money laundering and terrorist financing (Egmont Group, 2019). The UAE also cooperates with Interpol and other international law enforcement organizations to share information, best practices, and resources for combating organized crime and other illicit activities (Interpol, 2019).

The UAE has also signed Mutual Legal Assistance Treaties (MLATs) and extradition agreements with several countries to enhance international cooperation in criminal matters. These agreements allow the UAE to request and provide assistance in investigations, prosecutions, and other legal proceedings related to transnational organized crime and other offenses (U.S. Department of State, 2020).

While the UAE has made considerable progress in enhancing its law enforcement capacity, there is still room for improvement. The country should continue to invest in capacity-building programs for its law enforcement agencies, regulatory authorities, and judiciary, as well as foster greater international cooperation to effectively combat organized crime and other illicit activities.

The UAE has taken further steps to enhance its law enforcement capacity by adopting a risk-based approach to supervision and compliance. The Central Bank of the UAE has issued guidelines for financial institutions and designated non-financial businesses and professions to develop and implement risk-based anti-money laundering and countering the financing of terrorism (AML/CFT) programs. These guidelines emphasize the need for institutions to assess and mitigate the risks they face and to implement appropriate measures to prevent the misuse of their services for money laundering and terrorist financing (UAE Central Bank, 2020).

To bolster its efforts in combating human trafficking, the UAE has established a National Committee to Combat Human Trafficking (NCCHT) to coordinate and oversee the implementation of its anti-trafficking strategy. The NCCHT is responsible for developing and implementing policies, raising public awareness, and ensuring the provision of support services to victims of human trafficking (U.S. Department of State, 2020).

The UAE has also made strides in improving the transparency of its financial sector, such as with the introduction of the Economic Substance Regulations (ESR) in 2019. The ESR requires businesses to demonstrate that they are carrying out substantial economic activities within the UAE, thereby helping to prevent the misuse of the country's financial system for money laundering and other illicit activities (Ministry of Finance, 2019).

Despite these efforts, challenges remain, including the need to enhance the effectiveness of the FIU and AMLSCU as well as improve coordination among various law enforcement agencies, regulatory authorities, and the judiciary in the investigation and prosecution of organized crime and other illicit activities.

3. Challenges Faced by the UAE in Combating Organized Crime

Despite the UAE's concerted efforts to address organized crime, the country still faces several challenges in its fight against these criminal networks. Some of the key issues include:

a. Evolving Threats: As organized crime networks become more sophisticated and adaptive, the UAE must continually update its law enforcement strategies and tools to stay ahead of these evolving threats (Europol, 2018). Criminal organizations are constantly developing new techniques to evade detection and exploit vulnerabilities in the system. To effectively combat these threats, the UAE must invest in advanced technologies, enhance intelligence-gathering capabilities, and promote innovation in its law enforcement practices.

b. Limited Resources: While the UAE has made significant investments in its law enforcement capacity, it must continue to allocate sufficient resources to effectively combat organized crime (IMF, 2017). This includes not only financial resources but also human resources, such as well-trained personnel and specialized units dedicated to addressing different aspects of organized crime. Additionally, the UAE should prioritize international cooperation and information-sharing initiatives to leverage the expertise and resources of other countries in the global fight against organized crime.

c. Corruption: Organized crime networks often exploit corruption within the government and law enforcement institutions to further their criminal activities, presenting an ongoing challenge for the UAE in its fight against these groups (Shelley, 2014). Corruption can undermine the effectiveness of law enforcement efforts and provide opportunities for criminal organizations to infiltrate and co-opt public officials, thereby weakening the nation's overall ability to address organized crime. To counter this issue, the UAE must prioritize transparency and accountability in its public institutions, implement robust anti-corruption measures, and foster a culture of integrity and professionalism within its law enforcement agencies.

d. Legal and Regulatory Framework: While the UAE has enacted strict legislation to address various aspects of organized crime, the nation must ensure that its legal and regulatory framework remains up-to-date and comprehensive. This includes regularly reviewing and updating existing laws and regulations, closing any loopholes that may be exploited by criminal organizations, and adopting best practices from other jurisdictions.

In conclusion, the UAE faces several challenges in its fight against organized crime, including evolving threats, limited resources, corruption, and the need for a robust legal and regulatory framework. By addressing these challenges and maintaining a strong commitment to combating organized crime, the UAE can preserve its security, stability, and reputation as a safe and attractive destination for business and investment.

B. International Cooperation and Information Sharing

1.   Regional and Global Partnerships

Recognizing the transnational nature of organized crime, the UAE has actively engaged in international cooperation with other countries and regional organizations to combat drug cartels and mafia organizations (Europol, 2018). This includes participating in joint operations and information-sharing initiatives with organizations such as Interpol, Europol, and the Gulf Cooperation Council (GCC) to target organized crime networks and disrupt their activities (Al Tamimi & Company, 2018).

Interpol: The UAE collaborates with Interpol, the world's largest international police organization, to exchange intelligence, coordinate joint operations, and provide training and technical assistance in the fight against organized crime. Interpol's global network and databases enable the UAE to access and share critical information on criminals, criminal organizations, and their activities, which is essential for effective law enforcement efforts.

Europol: The UAE also cooperates with Europol, the European Union's law enforcement agency, to tackle organized crime networks that span across Europe and the Middle East. This collaboration includes sharing information on criminal activities such as drug trafficking, money laundering, and human trafficking, as well as participating in joint investigations and operations targeting organized crime groups.

Gulf Cooperation Council (GCC): The UAE is an active member of the GCC, a regional organization that fosters political, economic, and security cooperation among its six member states. The GCC provides a platform for the UAE to collaborate with its neighbors in the Gulf region on matters related to organized crime, such as sharing intelligence, conducting joint operations, and harmonizing legal frameworks.

Bilateral Agreements: The UAE has signed numerous bilateral agreements with other countries to facilitate cooperation in the fight against organized crime. These agreements encompass matters such as mutual legal assistance, extradition, and joint operations, enabling the UAE and its partners to effectively address the cross-border nature of organized crime.

Participation in International Forums: The UAE actively participates in various international forums and initiatives focused on combating organized crime, such as the United Nations Office on Drugs and Crime (UNODC), the Financial Action Task Force (FATF), and the Global Initiative against Transnational Organized Crime. These forums provide an opportunity for the UAE to share best practices, learn from other countries' experiences, and develop joint strategies to address the complex challenges posed by organized crime.

2. Mutual Legal Assistance

The UAE has also sought to strengthen its mutual legal assistance (MLA) relationships with other countries, facilitating the exchange of information and evidence related to criminal investigations and prosecutions (FATF, 2020). These MLA agreements enable the UAE to collaborate more effectively with foreign law enforcement agencies in pursuing organized crime networks and their members (IMF, 2017).

Purpose of Mutual Legal Assistance

Mutual legal assistance is a vital tool for countries to cooperate in the investigation, prosecution, and suppression of transnational criminal activities, such as drug trafficking, money laundering, and human trafficking (UNODC, 2012). By establishing MLA agreements with other nations, the UAE can request and provide assistance in various forms, including:

- Obtaining evidence and testimony
- Executing search and seizure operations
- Tracing and freezing assets
- Facilitating the extradition of criminals
- MLA Agreements and Regional Cooperation

The UAE has signed MLA agreements with several countries, including the United States, the United Kingdom, India, and Pakistan (U.S. Department of State, 2021). These agreements create a legal framework for the UAE and its partners to share information, resources, and expertise in the fight against organized crime.

Additionally, as a member of the Gulf Cooperation Council (GCC), the UAE benefits from the GCC's regional framework for mutual legal assistance, which aims to enhance cooperation among its member states in criminal matters (GCC, 2017).

Challenges and Opportunities in MLA

While the UAE's efforts to strengthen its mutual legal assistance relationships are commendable, there are still challenges to overcome. Some of these challenges include:

- Varying legal systems and procedures among countries can create obstacles to effective cooperation (UNODC, 2012).

- Delays in processing MLA requests can hinder timely investigations and prosecutions (FATF, 2020).
- Concerns about the protection of personal data and privacy may limit the extent of information sharing (IMF, 2017).

To address these challenges, the UAE should:

- Continue engaging in bilateral and multilateral dialogues to harmonize legal frameworks and procedures.
- Streamline the process of responding to MLA requests, ensuring timely and efficient cooperation.
- Develop and implement robust data protection measures that balance the need for information sharing with privacy concerns.

C. Prevention and Public Awareness Programs

1. Public Education Campaigns

To raise public awareness about the dangers posed by organized crime and to promote a culture of lawfulness, the UAE has implemented various public education campaigns (UNODC, 2016). These campaigns target various aspects of organized crime, such as drug abuse, human trafficking, and financial crimes, and are designed to educate the public about the risks associated with these activities and how to report suspected criminal activity (Europol, 2018).

Examples of these campaigns include the annual Anti-Drug Awareness Month, which aims to raise awareness about the dangers of drug use and addiction, and the annual National Human Trafficking Awareness Campaign, which seeks to increase public understanding of the issue and encourage people to report suspected cases (UAE Ministry of Interior, 2019).

2. Community Engagement Initiatives

In addition to public education campaigns, the UAE has engaged in community engagement initiatives aimed at preventing organized crime and fostering public vigilance against these threats (UNODC, 2016). These initiatives include partnerships with local community organizations, schools, and religious institutions to promote awareness of organized crime and its negative impacts on society (IMF, 2017).

One example of this is the establishment of the Hemaya (Protection) Foundation, which focuses on promoting community awareness of drug-related issues and supporting drug rehabilitation efforts in the UAE (Hemaya Foundation, 2020). By fostering a strong sense of community involvement and responsibility, these initiatives help to build resilience against organized crime and encourage citizens to actively participate in the fight against these criminal networks (UNODC, 2016).

3. Private Sector Collaboration

Recognizing the crucial role that the private sector plays in combating organized crime, particularly in areas such as financial crimes and cybercrime, the UAE has sought to strengthen its partnerships with businesses and financial institutions (FATF, 2020). This collaboration involves sharing information, best practices, and resources to enhance the private sector's ability to detect and report suspicious activities, thereby making it more difficult for organized crime networks to exploit the financial system and conduct their operations (IMF, 2017).

For instance, the UAE Central Bank regularly conducts workshops and training sessions for financial institutions on anti-money laundering (AML) and countering the financing of terrorism (CFT) measures, helping them to identify and report suspicious transactions (UAE Central Bank, 2021). Additionally, the UAE has established the National Cyber Security Council, which brings together representatives from the public and private sectors to enhance the nation's cybersecurity capabilities and protect against cyber threats, including those from organized crime groups (UAE National Cyber Security Council, 2020).

4. Youth Engagement and Education Programs

The UAE has also placed a strong emphasis on engaging and educating the youth about the dangers of organized crime and the importance of upholding the rule of law (UNODC, 2016). By targeting the younger generation, these initiatives aim to create a long-lasting impact and foster a future generation of citizens who are better equipped to resist the temptations of criminal activities.

For example, the UAE's Ministry of Education has introduced programs in schools to educate students about the risks associated with drug use, cybercrimes, and human trafficking (UAE Ministry of Education, 2018). These programs are designed to help students develop critical thinking skills and learn how to protect themselves and their communities from the threats posed by organized crime.

5.   Capacity Building and Training Programs for Law Enforcement

The UAE government has also invested in capacity-building and training programs for law enforcement agencies to enhance their ability to combat organized crime (UNODC, 2016). These programs provide officers with the necessary knowledge and skills to effectively investigate and prosecute organized crime cases, as well as to collaborate with other domestic and international law enforcement agencies.

For instance, the UAE has established the Dubai Police Academy, which offers specialized training courses in areas such as financial crime investigation, cybercrime, and drug enforcement (Dubai Police Academy, 2021). Furthermore, the UAE regularly participates in joint training exercises and workshops with international partners, such as Interpol and the United Nations Office on Drugs and Crime, to share knowledge and expertise in the fight against organized crime (Interpol, 2020).

In conclusion, the UAE's efforts to combat organized crime encompass a comprehensive approach that includes prevention, public awareness programs, community engagement initiatives, private sector collaboration, youth engagement, and capacity building for law enforcement. By continuing to invest in these multifaceted efforts, the UAE can further strengthen its resilience against organized crime and ensure the safety and security of its citizens.

The UAE has put a lot of effort into battling the growing threat from organized crime, including drug cartels and mafia groups. Through a combination of law enforcement strategies, international cooperation, and prevention and public awareness programs, the UAE has demonstrated its commitment to addressing this complex and evolving challenge. However, it is essential for the UAE to continue to invest in its law enforcement capacity, strengthen its international partnerships, and engage its citizens and the private sector in the fight against organized crime to effectively mitigate the risks and impacts associated with these criminal networks.

THE FUTURE OF ORGANIZED CRIME IN THE UAE

A. Emerging Trends and Challenges

1. Cybercrime and the Digital Landscape

As technology continues to evolve, organized crime networks have started to adapt their methods and strategies to take advantage of new digital platforms and tools (Europol, 2020). Cybercrime, including online fraud, identity theft, and hacking, poses a significant challenge for the UAE, as it allows criminal organizations to carry out their activities remotely and with a reduced risk of detection (IMF, 2019).

Cybercrime, including online fraud, identity theft, and hacking, poses a significant challenge for the UAE, as it allows mafia and criminal organizations to carry out their activities remotely and with a reduced risk of detection (Buchanan, 2020). The rapid growth of the digital economy and the widespread adoption of new technologies in the country have created numerous opportunities for cybercriminals to exploit vulnerabilities in information systems and networks for illicit purposes (Alazab, 2021).

One of the primary tactics employed by mafia and criminal organizations in the UAE is online fraud, which encompasses a wide range of activities such as phishing, social engineering, and investment scams (Europol, 2020). These schemes often involve the use of sophisticated techniques to deceive individuals and businesses into revealing sensitive information or transferring funds to accounts controlled by criminals (Kaspersky Lab, 2021).

Identity theft is another significant issue, as it enables criminals to obtain personal and financial information from unsuspecting victims, which can then be used to commit various types of fraud, including credit card fraud, bank fraud, and tax fraud (Alazab, 2021). In some cases, criminal organizations may also use stolen identities to facilitate money laundering, human trafficking, and other illicit activities (Buchanan, 2020).

Hacking poses an additional threat, as it allows mafia and criminal organizations to gain unauthorized access to computer systems, networks, and data for a variety of purposes, including espionage, sabotage, and financial gain (Europol, 2020). Cybercriminals may also engage in the theft of intellectual property and trade secrets, which can have significant economic and national security implications for the UAE (Kaspersky Lab, 2021).

To effectively combat cybercrime and protect the integrity of its digital economy, the UAE needs to adopt a multi-faceted approach that includes strengthening legal frameworks, enhancing law enforcement capacity, investing in cybersecurity infrastructure, promoting public-private partnerships, and raising public awareness (Choo, 2021).

In addition to the aforementioned measures, international cooperation is a crucial aspect of the UAE's efforts to combat cybercrime, as criminal networks often operate across national borders (Choo, 2021). By participating in global initiatives, such as the Budapest Convention on Cybercrime, the UAE can collaborate with other countries to share information, coordinate law enforcement efforts, and develop joint strategies to address the challenges posed by mafia and criminal organizations in the cyber domain (Council of Europe, 2001).

Furthermore, the UAE should invest in research and development to foster innovation in cybersecurity technologies and solutions. Supporting academic institutions and research centers in the country can lead to the development of cutting-edge tools and methodologies that can be used to detect, prevent, and respond to cybercrime threats more effectively (Buchanan, 2020).

Educational initiatives aimed at promoting digital literacy and teaching students about safe online practices are another important component of the UAE's efforts to combat cybercrime. By incorporating cybersecurity education into school curriculums and providing resources for teachers, the UAE can empower future generations to become responsible digital citizens and reduce their vulnerability to cyber threats (Choo, 2021).

2. Exploitation of Cryptocurrencies

The rapid development and widespread adoption of cryptocurrencies have provided new opportunities for criminal organizations to engage in illicit activities. In the UAE, the use of cryptocurrencies by the mafia and other criminal networks has become a growing concern, as these digital assets can facilitate money laundering, terrorist financing, and other forms of financial crime (Castillo & Smith, 2023).

One of the primary advantages of cryptocurrencies for criminal organizations is their ability to bypass traditional financial institutions and regulations, thus providing a higher degree of anonymity and reducing the risk of detection (Choo, 2021). Additionally, the decentralized nature of cryptocurrencies enables these organizations to carry out cross-border transactions quickly and with minimal transaction costs, further complicating the efforts of law enforcement agencies to monitor and trace the flow of illicit funds (Europol, 2021).

The UAE has become an attractive destination for criminal organizations seeking to exploit cryptocurrencies due to its advanced technological infrastructure, relatively lax regulation of digital assets, and the presence of numerous cryptocurrency exchanges and other service providers (Hutchings & Guala, 2017). In response to these challenges, the UAE government has taken steps to strengthen the regulatory framework for cryptocurrencies, including the introduction of the Virtual Asset Regulation in 2020, which requires cryptocurrency service providers to obtain licenses and comply with anti-money laundering (AML) and counter-terrorism financing (CTF) requirements (UAE Central Bank, 2020).

Despite these efforts, the exploitation of cryptocurrencies by the mafia and criminal organizations in the UAE remains a significant challenge. Criminal networks have been found to use cryptocurrencies to facilitate the trade of illegal goods and services, such as drugs, weapons, and counterfeit products, as well as to launder the proceeds of their criminal activities (Castillo & Smith, 2023).

In order to effectively combat the exploitation of cryptocurrencies by criminal organizations in the UAE, it is essential to enhance the capacity of law enforcement agencies, regulators, and the judiciary to understand, investigate, and prosecute cases involving the illicit use of digital assets. This may involve the provision of specialized training, the development of new investigative techniques and tools, and greater international cooperation and information sharing (Europol, 2021).

Moreover, the UAE government should consider introducing additional regulatory measures to enhance transparency and accountability in the cryptocurrency sector, such as implementing strict customer due diligence (CDD) requirements for cryptocurrency service providers, requiring the reporting of suspicious transactions, and establishing mechanisms for the effective supervision and enforcement of these regulations (Choo, 2021).

To further address the issue of mafia and criminal organizations exploiting cryptocurrencies in the UAE, the government should also promote public-private partnerships to facilitate greater collaboration between law enforcement agencies, regulators, and the cryptocurrency industry. This could involve the establishment of joint working groups, the sharing of best practices, and the development of new initiatives to detect and prevent illicit activities involving digital assets (FATF, 2021).

Public awareness campaigns can also play a crucial role in countering the exploitation of cryptocurrencies by criminal networks in the UAE. By raising awareness about the risks associated with the illicit use of digital assets and promoting a culture of compliance within the cryptocurrency sector, the UAE government can help foster a more secure and responsible environment for the development and use of these technologies (Choo, 2021).

Additionally, international cooperation and information sharing are critical components of any effective strategy to combat the exploitation of cryptocurrencies by the mafia and criminal organizations. The UAE should actively participate in global efforts to develop common standards and best practices for the regulation and supervision of digital assets, as well as enhance cross-border cooperation and coordination among law enforcement agencies, regulators, and the cryptocurrency industry (FATF, 2021).

3. Transnational Networks

Organized crime networks have become increasingly transnational, often collaborating with other criminal organizations from different countries to expand their operations and evade law enforcement (Europol, 2020). This trend presents a significant challenge for the UAE, as it requires greater international cooperation and coordination to effectively combat these increasingly complex and interconnected networks (IMF, 2017).

The United Arab Emirates (UAE) has increasingly become a hub for mafia and criminal organizations' transnational networks due to its strategic location, rapid economic development, and global business connections (Inteldrop, 2023). These criminal networks exploit the UAE's infrastructure and financial systems to facilitate a range of illegal activities, including drug trafficking, money laundering, human trafficking, and arms smuggling (Cockayne, 2011).

Transnational criminal organizations often establish complex networks spanning multiple countries and continents, allowing them to operate efficiently and evade law enforcement detection (Shelley, 2014). The UAE's position as a major transportation and financial hub in the Middle East makes it an attractive destination for criminal networks seeking to expand their operations and launder illicit proceeds (Inteldrop, 2023).

One of the most notorious examples of a transnational criminal network operating in the UAE is the Sinaloa Cartel, a powerful Mexican drug trafficking organization with a significant presence in the country (Inteldrop, 2023). The cartel is known for smuggling large quantities of narcotics, such as cocaine and heroin, through the UAE and other countries in the Middle East before ultimately distributing the drugs in Europe and other markets (Serrano, 2018).

Money laundering is another significant concern in the UAE, as criminal organizations exploit the country's financial systems and real estate market to launder illicit funds (Carnegie Endowment, 2020). For example, the 'Ndrangheta, a powerful Italian mafia organization, has been linked to numerous money laundering schemes involving the UAE, including the purchase of luxury properties in Dubai using proceeds from drug trafficking and other criminal activities (OCCRP, 2020).

Human trafficking is another issue that has been associated with transnational criminal networks operating in the UAE. Criminal organizations from various countries, including India, Pakistan, and Eastern Europe, have been known to exploit the UAE's migrant worker population, subjecting them to forced labor, sexual exploitation, and other forms of abuse (US Department of State, 2020).

The UAE needs to take a multifaceted approach to combat the threat that transnational criminal networks pose, which includes strengthening legal frameworks, enhancing law enforcement capability, improving international cooperation, and raising public awareness (Cockayne, 2011).

The UAE has made efforts to strengthen its legal frameworks by enacting comprehensive legislation aimed at combating organized crime, such as Federal Law No. 7 of 2014 on Combating Terrorism Offenses (UAE Government, 2014). This law criminalizes a wide range of activities associated with transnational criminal networks, including terrorism financing, money laundering, and human trafficking (UAE Government, 2014).

Enhancing law enforcement capacity is another crucial aspect of the UAE's efforts to combat transnational criminal networks. This includes providing specialized training for law enforcement officers, establishing dedicated units to investigate organized crime, and promoting inter-agency collaboration (Cockayne, 2011).

International cooperation is essential for effectively addressing the challenges posed by transnational criminal networks, as these organizations often operate across national borders (Shelley, 2014). The UAE needs to engage in greater collaboration with other countries, share intelligence, and participate in global initiatives aimed at combating organized crime, such as the United Nations Convention against Transnational Organized Crime (UNODC, 2000).

Promoting public awareness is another essential component of the UAE's strategy to combat transnational criminal networks. By raising awareness about the dangers posed by these organizations and educating the public about how to identify and report suspicious activities, the UAE can foster a culture of vigilance and resilience that makes it more difficult for criminal networks to operate within its borders (Cockayne, 2011).

The private sector also plays a crucial role in combating transnational criminal networks in the UAE. Companies should be encouraged to adopt robust anti-money laundering (AML) and compliance programs, conduct thorough due diligence on their business partners, and report any suspicious transactions to the relevant authorities (Carnegie Endowment, 2020). Financial institutions, in particular, should be held to high standards of transparency and accountability to prevent them from being exploited by criminal organizations seeking to launder illicit proceeds (Cockayne, 2011).

In addition to these measures, the UAE should continue to invest in cutting-edge technologies and analytical tools that can help law enforcement agencies track, analyze, and disrupt the activities of transnational criminal networks (Shelley, 2014). This includes the use of artificial intelligence, machine learning, and big data analytics to identify patterns and trends in criminal activity, as well as the development of secure information-sharing platforms that enable real-time collaboration among law enforcement agencies both within the UAE and internationally (Cockayne, 2011).

By adopting a comprehensive and proactive approach to combating transnational criminal networks, the UAE can effectively mitigate the risks associated with organized crime and protect its national security, economic interests, and the well-being of its citizens.

B. Potential Solutions and Strategies

1. Strengthening International Cooperation

To address the growing threat of transnational organized crime, the UAE will need to further strengthen its international partnerships and collaborations with other countries and regional organizations (Europol, 2020). This may involve participating in joint operations, sharing intelligence, and working together to develop best practices and policies to combat organized crime (FATF, 2020). Additionally, enhancing cooperation with organizations such as Interpol, Europol, and the Gulf Cooperation Council (GCC) can improve the effectiveness of multinational efforts against organized crime networks (Al Tamimi & Company, 2018).

2. Investing in Law Enforcement Capacity and Training

As organized crime networks become more sophisticated and technologically advanced, the UAE must invest in enhancing its law enforcement capacity and providing specialized training for its officers (IMF, 2017). This includes developing expertise in areas such as cybercrime, financial crimes, and intelligence analysis, as well as equipping law enforcement agencies with the necessary tools and resources to effectively combat organized crime (Europol, 2020). Fostering cross-agency collaboration and information-sharing can further improve the efficiency and effectiveness of law enforcement efforts against organized crime (Hutchings & Guala, 2017).

3. Implementing Targeted Prevention and Awareness Programs

To prevent the growth and spread of organized crime, the UAE should continue to implement targeted prevention and public awareness programs that address the root causes of these criminal activities (UNODC, 2016). This may involve working with local communities, schools, and religious institutions to promote a culture of lawfulness and provide education and support for those at risk of becoming involved in organized crime (IMF, 2017). Furthermore, leveraging public-private partnerships can help raise awareness about the dangers of organized crime and foster a sense of community responsibility in combatting these threats (Alhyas, Elarabi, & AlGhaferi, 2015).

4. Strengthening Anti-Money Laundering and Countering the Financing of Terrorism Measures

Given the crucial role that money laundering and terrorism financing play in enabling organized crime, the UAE must continue to strengthen its anti-money laundering (AML) and countering the financing of terrorism (CFT) measures (FATF, 2020). This includes enhancing its legal framework, implementing risk-based supervision of financial institutions and designated non-financial businesses and professions, and increasing cooperation and information sharing between relevant domestic authorities and international partners (IMF, 2017).

5. Combating Corruption

As corruption facilitates organized crime activities, the UAE should continue to address this issue through effective anti-corruption measures, such as promoting transparency and accountability, implementing robust whistleblower protection laws, and fostering a culture of integrity within public institutions (Transparency International, 2019). By tackling corruption head-on, the UAE can weaken the influence of organized crime networks and reduce their ability to infiltrate and co-opt government and law enforcement institutions (Shelley, 2014).

6. Enhancing Cybersecurity Measures

With the increasing use of technology by organized crime groups, the UAE must prioritize enhancing its cybersecurity measures (Europol, 2020). This includes developing a robust cybersecurity infrastructure, creating specialized law enforcement units to combat cybercrime, and raising awareness about cyber threats among the public and private sectors (IMF, 2017). By building a strong cybersecurity framework, the UAE can better protect its citizens and businesses from cyberattacks and disrupt the operations of criminal networks that rely on digital technologies (Europol, 2020).

7. Fostering Public-Private Partnerships

Public-private partnerships can play a crucial role in the UAE's efforts to combat organized crime, particularly in areas such as financial crimes and cybercrime (FATF, 2020). By engaging with businesses, financial institutions, and technology companies, the UAE can leverage their expertise, resources, and information to better detect and report suspicious activities related to organized crime (IMF, 2017). These partnerships can also help develop innovative solutions and technologies to counter the evolving threats posed by organized crime networks (Europol, 2020).

8. Addressing Social and Economic Inequalities

Social and economic inequalities can contribute to the growth and spread of organized crime, as marginalized and vulnerable populations may be more susceptible to recruitment by criminal networks (UNODC, 2016). The UAE should continue to address these inequalities through inclusive policies, such as providing access to quality education, healthcare, and employment opportunities for all citizens (IMF, 2017). By fostering social and economic stability, the UAE can reduce the appeal of organized crime and create a more resilient society (UNODC, 2016).

9. Enhancing Intelligence and Data Analysis Capabilities

The ability to collect, analyze, and share intelligence and data is essential in the fight against organized crime (Europol, 2020). The UAE should invest in advanced analytical tools and technologies, as well as training for its intelligence and law enforcement personnel, to enhance its capabilities in this area (IMF, 2017). By developing a strong intelligence and data analysis infrastructure, the UAE can more effectively identify, track, and disrupt organized crime networks operating within its borders and beyond (Europol, 2020).

10. Establishing Specialized Courts and Prosecutorial Units

To improve the effectiveness and efficiency of the UAE's criminal justice system in addressing organized crime, the establishment of specialized courts and prosecutorial units focused on organized crime cases may be beneficial (UNODC, 2016). These specialized units can provide the necessary expertise, resources, and focus to successfully prosecute complex organized crime cases, thereby enhancing the UAE's ability to hold organized crime networks accountable and deter potential criminals (IMF, 2017).

By implementing these strategies, the UAE can strengthen its response to organized crime and work towards ensuring the safety and security of its citizens, businesses, and institutions. The ongoing efforts to combat organized crime must be comprehensive and coordinated, involving a wide range of stakeholders and partners both domestically and internationally.

C. The Role of Technology and Innovation

1. Leveraging Advanced Technologies for Detection and Prevention

The UAE can harness the power of technology and innovation to develop new tools and methods for detecting and preventing organized crime (Europol, 2020). This includes utilizing advanced data analytics, artificial intelligence, and machine learning algorithms to identify patterns and trends in criminal activities (IMF, 2019). By leveraging these technologies, law enforcement agencies can enhance their ability to track and disrupt organized crime networks more effectively. Additionally, investing in cutting-edge surveillance systems and biometric identification technologies can help improve the accuracy and efficiency of investigations and border security (IMF, 2019).

2. Developing Cybersecurity Strategies

As cybercrime becomes an increasingly significant threat, the UAE will need to develop comprehensive cybersecurity strategies and policies to protect its critical infrastructure and citizens from online attacks (IMF, 2019). This includes working closely with the private sector and international partners to share information, best practices, and resources for combating cybercrime and ensuring the security of digital networks and systems (Europol, 2020). By establishing a strong cybersecurity framework and fostering collaboration among relevant stakeholders, the UAE can better protect itself from cyber threats and hinder the operations of organized crime groups that rely on digital technologies.

3.   Regulating Cryptocurrencies and Emerging Technologies

In order to address the challenges posed by cryptocurrencies and other emerging technologies, the UAE must develop regulatory frameworks that can adapt to the rapidly changing landscape (FATF, 2020). This may involve creating clear guidelines for the use of cryptocurrencies, implementing robust anti-money laundering and counter-terrorism financing measures for digital currencies, and working with international partners to establish global standards and best practices for regulating these new technologies (IMF, 2019). By proactively addressing the potential risks associated with cryptocurrencies and emerging technologies, the UAE can mitigate the opportunities for organized crime networks to exploit these innovations for their illicit activities.

In conclusion, the future of organized crime in the UAE presents several challenges, including the growing role of technology and the increasing sophistication and transnational nature of criminal networks. However, by investing in its law enforcement capacity, strengthening international cooperation, and leveraging technology and innovation, the UAE can develop effective strategies to combat these threats and ensure the safety and security of its citizens. By adopting a proactive and adaptive approach to organized crime, the UAE can continue to build on its successes in this area and work towards a safer and more secure future.

D. The Road Ahead: Strengthening the UAE's Efforts Against Organized Crime

1.   Enhancing Public-Private Partnerships

The UAE should continue to foster strong public-private partnerships to address organized crime (IMF, 2017). By working closely with businesses, financial institutions, and technology companies, the government can leverage private sector expertise and resources to tackle various aspects of organized crime, such as money laundering, cybercrime, and human trafficking (FATF, 2020). Encouraging collaboration between law enforcement agencies and the private sector can lead to innovative solutions and improved information sharing, which is essential in the fight against organized crime networks.

2. Strengthening the Legal Framework

To further bolster its efforts against organized crime, the UAE should continue to strengthen its legal framework by reviewing and updating relevant laws and regulations (Europol, 2020). This may include adopting new legislation to address emerging threats, such as cybercrime and the use of cryptocurrencies, as well as enhancing existing laws to ensure they remain effective in the face of evolving criminal tactics (FATF, 2020). A robust legal framework is crucial for holding organized crime groups accountable and deterring potential offenders.

3. Encouraging Regional and Global Cooperation

Given the transnational nature of organized crime, the UAE should continue to prioritize regional and global cooperation in its efforts to combat these threats (Europol, 2020). This may entail cooperating closely with neighboring nations and regional organizations like the Gulf Cooperation Council (GCC), as well as taking part in global initiatives run by organizations like Interpol and the United Nations Office on Drugs and Crime (UNODC) (IMF, 2017). By actively engaging in international partnerships, the UAE can contribute to a more coordinated and effective global response to organized crime.

In summary, the UAE faces numerous challenges in its ongoing battle against organized crime. However, by investing in law enforcement capacity, strengthening international cooperation, leveraging technology and innovation, and enhancing its legal framework, the UAE can continue to make progress in addressing this issue. By adopting a comprehensive and strategic approach to organized crime, the UAE can help protect its citizens and maintain its reputation as a safe and secure nation.

CONCLUSION

A. The Significance of Addressing Organized Crime in the UAE

1. Protecting the UAE's Reputation and Economic
    Development

Organized crime poses a significant threat to the UAE's reputation as a safe and stable country for business, investment, and tourism (IMF, 2017). By addressing organized crime, the UAE can protect its economic development and maintain its status as a global hub for trade, finance, and innovation (Europol, 2020). Failure to combat organized crime can have long-term implications for the country's growth and attractiveness to foreign investors and businesses (Al Tamimi & Company, 2018).

2. Ensuring the Safety and Security of the UAE's Citizens

The presence of organized crime networks can have devastating impacts on the safety and security of the UAE's citizens, as these groups engage in activities such as drug trafficking, human trafficking, and financial crimes that can cause significant harm to individuals and communities (UNODC, 2016). By combating organized crime, the UAE can help to ensure the well-being of its citizens and promote a culture of lawfulness and social cohesion (IMF, 2017). Effective efforts against organized crime contribute to the overall stability of the country and help create a safer environment for residents and visitors alike.

3. Upholding the Rule of Law and Strengthening Institutions

Organized crime can undermine the rule of law and weaken institutions, as criminal networks often exploit corruption and weaknesses within government and law enforcement agencies to further their activities (Shelley, 2014). By addressing organized crime, the UAE can strengthen its institutions and uphold the rule of law, ensuring that its legal and regulatory frameworks are robust and effective in protecting the country and its citizens from harm (FATF, 2020). A strong rule of law and institutional integrity are critical for fostering a climate of trust and accountability, which is essential for both the government and the private sector.

In conclusion, addressing organized crime in the UAE is essential for protecting its reputation, ensuring the safety and security of its citizens, and upholding the rule of law. By investing in law enforcement capacity, strengthening international cooperation, leveraging technology and innovation, and enhancing its legal framework, the UAE can develop effective strategies to combat these threats and maintain its position as a safe and prosperous nation.

B. Future Outlook and Recommendations

As the UAE continues to grow and evolve, its approach to combating organized crime must also adapt and improve. To effectively tackle the various challenges posed by organized crime, the UAE should consider the following recommendations:

1. Enhance Data Collection and Analysis

Efforts to combat organized crime in the UAE can benefit from enhanced data collection and analysis capabilities. By implementing robust data collection systems and utilizing advanced analytics, the UAE can better understand the extent of organized crime within its borders and develop targeted strategies to address specific issues (Europol, 2020). Improved data collection and analysis can also facilitate more effective collaboration and information sharing with international partners.

2. Promote Public-Private Partnerships

Public-private partnerships can play a crucial role in combating organized crime, particularly in areas such as financial crimes and cybercrime. By fostering collaboration between government agencies, private sector organizations, and civil society, the UAE can develop comprehensive strategies that address the various facets of organized crime and leverage the resources and expertise of all stakeholders (FATF, 2020).

3.   Strengthen Anti-Corruption Measures

To effectively combat organized crime, the UAE must also address corruption within its government and law enforcement agencies. Implementing strong anti-corruption measures, such as transparent procurement processes, robust whistleblower protection laws, and increased oversight of public officials, can help to reduce the opportunities for organized crime networks to exploit vulnerabilities within the system (IMF, 2017).

4.   Foster Regional Cooperation

Given the transnational nature of organized crime, regional cooperation is essential for addressing this issue effectively. The UAE should continue to work closely with its neighbors in the Gulf Cooperation Council (GCC) and other regional organizations to develop joint strategies, share information, and coordinate efforts to combat organized crime networks that operate across national borders (Europol, 2020).

By implementing these recommendations and continuing to invest in its law enforcement capacity, international cooperation, and technological capabilities, the UAE can make significant strides in addressing the challenges posed by organized crime. In doing so, the nation will be better positioned to protect its reputation, ensure the safety and security of its citizens, and maintain its status as a global hub for trade, finance, and innovation.

C. The Broader Implications for the International Community

1.   Enhancing Global Security and Stability

Organized crime networks frequently operate transnationally, engaging in activities that significantly impact global security and stability (Europol, 2020). Although the UAE has taken some steps to address organized crime within its borders, its efforts have been insufficient to make a meaningful impact on global security and stability. The disruption of these networks is crucial for reducing the flow of illicit goods, money, and people across borders (IMF, 2017).

One of the main reasons for the UAE's inadequate response to organized crime is its reluctance to acknowledge and address the extent of the problem within its jurisdiction. This lack of transparency hinders both national and international efforts to tackle organized crime networks and their activities (Europol, 2020). The UAE must take a more proactive approach by acknowledging the scope of the problem and implementing comprehensive measures to combat these criminal networks.

Additionally, allegations of human rights violations, corruption, and a lack of equitable access to the legal system have undermined the UAE's efforts to combat organized crime. These issues undermine the country's credibility and its ability to contribute effectively to global security and stability (Stirling, 2023). To address these concerns, the UAE must prioritize the rule of law, transparency, and respect for human rights while combating organized crime.

Moreover, the UAE has not fully leveraged its strategic location and resources to contribute to international efforts against organized crime. The country's position as a global financial and transportation hub makes it an attractive target for organized crime networks seeking to smuggle illicit goods and launder money (IMF, 2017). To stop transnational criminal networks from taking advantage of its territory, the UAE needs to strengthen its regulatory framework and enforcement mechanisms.

Furthermore, the UAE must actively engage with regional and global partners to strengthen international cooperation and information sharing in the fight against organized crime. The country can enhance its contribution to global security and stability by participating more actively in joint operations, capacity-building initiatives, and intelligence sharing with other countries (FATF, 2020).

The UAE's efforts to address organized crime within its borders have been inadequate, hindering its ability to contribute effectively to global security and stability. To address these shortcomings, the UAE must acknowledge the extent of the problem, prioritize the rule of law and human rights, strengthen its regulatory framework and enforcement mechanisms, and actively engage with regional and global partners. These efforts will not only help the UAE become a more effective contributor to global security and stability but also improve its internal security and the well-being of its citizens.

2. Encouraging International Cooperation and Information Sharing

As organized crime networks become increasingly sophisticated and interconnected, international cooperation and information sharing among countries are essential to combating these threats (Europol, 2020). Although the UAE has taken some steps to address organized crime within its borders, there is still room for improvement in fostering greater collaboration and openness with regional and global partners. Strengthening these efforts is vital for effectively tackling the complex and evolving challenges posed by organized crime networks (FATF, 2020).

One area where the UAE can improve its efforts is by establishing more robust channels for intelligence sharing with other countries. While the UAE participates in various international forums and organizations, there is a need for more proactive and transparent engagement in sharing intelligence, best practices, and resources with partner nations. This includes working closely with regional partners such as the Gulf Cooperation Council (GCC) and international organizations such as Interpol, Europol, and the United Nations Office on Drugs and Crime (UNODC) (Europol, 2020).

Another crucial aspect where the UAE can enhance its cooperation is in joint operations and capacity building. Participating in multinational task forces and initiatives, such as the Combined Maritime Forces, can help the UAE contribute to a more coordinated and effective regional response to organized crime. Additionally, the UAE can provide training and technical assistance to law enforcement agencies in neighboring countries to build capacity and improve their ability to address organized crime networks (FATF, 2020).

Furthermore, the UAE should take a more proactive role in promoting regional and international legal frameworks and agreements to combat organized crime. This includes ratifying and implementing relevant international conventions, such as the United Nations Convention against Transnational Organized Crime and its protocols, and actively participating in the development and implementation of regional strategies and action plans to address organized crime (UNODC, 2016).

Lastly, the UAE must also address its internal challenges, such as corruption and a lack of transparency, which can hinder effective international cooperation and information sharing. Strengthening anti-corruption measures and promoting transparency in both the public and private sectors will help build trust and credibility with international partners, paving the way for more effective collaboration and information exchange (FATF, 2020).

While the UAE has made some progress in addressing organized crime, it must take more proactive and critical steps to encourage international cooperation and information sharing. By strengthening intelligence sharing channels, participating in joint operations, promoting regional and international legal frameworks, and addressing internal challenges, the UAE can contribute to more effective global efforts to combat organized crime networks and their complex and evolving threats.

3. Promoting Sustainable Development and Social Progress

Organized crime poses a considerable challenge to sustainable development and social progress, as it undermines economic growth, fuels corruption, and exacerbates social inequality (UNODC, 2016). While the UAE has made efforts to address organized crime within its borders, there remains a need for more critical evaluation and action to effectively combat the negative consequences of these criminal networks on sustainable development.

The UAE's rapid economic growth and development have attracted various organized crime networks seeking to exploit the country's financial systems and infrastructure for illicit purposes. These criminal networks engage in activities such as money laundering, drug trafficking, and human trafficking, which not only hinder the country's economic progress but also contribute to social inequality and corruption (IMF, 2017). The UAE government must recognize the urgency of this issue and implement comprehensive strategies to address the root causes of organized crime and its impact on sustainable development and social progress.

One crucial area where the UAE's efforts fall short is in transparency and anti-corruption measures. While the country has implemented some anti-money laundering and counter-terrorism financing regulations, more robust mechanisms are needed to combat corruption and increase transparency in the public and private sectors. This includes strengthening the legal framework and establishing independent oversight bodies to monitor and enforce anti-corruption measures (UNODC, 2016).

Additionally, the UAE must address the social factors that contribute to the growth and spread of organized crime, such as poverty, a lack of education, and limited access to social services. By investing in social programs and targeted interventions, the UAE can reduce the vulnerability of marginalized communities and individuals who may be at risk of becoming involved in criminal activities. These efforts will not only help to disrupt the networks of organized crime but also contribute to greater social equity and inclusion in the country.

Furthermore, the UAE must enhance its cooperation and collaboration with regional and international partners to effectively combat organized crime networks that operate across borders. This includes sharing intelligence, best practices, and resources to dismantle these networks and disrupt their activities. By fostering stronger partnerships and alliances, the UAE can contribute to a more stable and secure international environment, promoting sustainable development and social progress globally (Europol, 2020).

While the UAE has made some progress in addressing organized crime, more critical and comprehensive efforts are needed to tackle the issue and its impact on sustainable development and social progress. By enhancing transparency, investing in social programs, and fostering international cooperation, the UAE can create a more just, equitable, and prosperous society for its citizens and contribute to global efforts to combat organized crime and promote sustainable development.

4. Addressing the UAE's Shortcomings in Rule of Law and Human Rights

Efforts to combat organized crime can have broader implications for the international community in terms of strengthening the rule of law and promoting respect for human rights (UNODC, 2016). Organized crime networks often thrive in environments where the rule of law is weak and human rights abuses are rampant, as they can exploit these vulnerabilities to further their activities (Shelley, 2014). However, the UAE's approach to combating organized crime has been criticized for its failure to adequately address human rights concerns and ensure equitable access to the legal process.

Despite its successes in addressing organized crime, the UAE has faced criticism for its human rights record and the lack of transparency within its legal system (Human Rights Watch, 2021). These shortcomings have raised concerns about the fairness and effectiveness of the UAE's efforts to combat organized crime, as well as the potential for human rights abuses to be perpetuated under the guise of national security and law enforcement (Amnesty International, 2020).

To address these concerns, the UAE should take several steps to strengthen the rule of law and uphold human rights within its borders. First, the UAE must ensure that its legal system is transparent and accessible, with due process protections in place for all individuals, regardless of their nationality or social status. This includes providing access to legal representation, ensuring fair and timely trials, and promoting the independence of the judiciary (Amnesty International, 2020).

Second, the UAE should address its human rights record by implementing policies and practices that respect and protect the rights of its citizens and residents. This includes addressing issues such as arbitrary detention, torture, and inhumane treatment of prisoners, as well as ensuring freedom of expression and association for all individuals (Human Rights Watch, 2021).

Finally, the UAE should work to create a more inclusive society by addressing social and economic inequalities that can contribute to the growth of organized crime networks. This includes promoting equal access to education, employment, and social services for all citizens and residents, as well as addressing issues such as human trafficking and labor exploitation (UNODC, 2016).

By addressing these shortcomings and implementing effective legal and regulatory frameworks, the UAE can contribute to global efforts to uphold the rule of law and protect human rights, setting a positive example for other countries to follow (IMF, 2017).

In a recent article on Detained in Dubai, Radha Stirling, the founder of the organization, comments on the arrest of British reality TV star Kaz Crossley in Dubai. Stirling emphasizes the need for greater awareness among tourists and expats about the UAE's strict laws, which may differ significantly from their home countries. She also highlights the importance of understanding cultural sensitivities and legal restrictions to avoid facing legal consequences while visiting or living in the country (Detained in Dubai, 2023).

5. Supporting Regional Stability and Development

Organized crime can pose significant threats to regional stability and development, particularly in areas where criminal networks have established strong footholds and engage in activities that undermine state authority and social cohesion (Europol, 2020). By addressing organized crime within its borders, the UAE can contribute to the stability and development of the broader Middle East region. This can be achieved through sharing best practices, providing assistance to neighboring countries, and participating in regional initiatives to combat organized crime (FATF, 2020). By doing so, the UAE can foster a more secure and prosperous regional environment, where countries can collaborate to promote peace, stability, and sustainable growth (IMF, 2017).

6. Facilitating a Global Response to Emerging Threats

As organized crime networks adapt to new technologies and develop innovative methods for conducting their activities, it is crucial for the international community to stay ahead of these emerging threats (Europol, 2020). The UAE's efforts to address organized crime, particularly in areas such as cybersecurity, digital currencies, and advanced surveillance technologies, can contribute to the development of a global response to these evolving challenges (IMF, 2019). By sharing its experiences, expertise, and innovative approaches, the UAE can help shape a more effective and coordinated international strategy to combat organized crime and protect the safety and security of people around the world (FATF, 2020).

In recent years, the United Arab Emirates (UAE) has become a prime target for cybercriminals and hackers seeking to exploit the country's growing digital infrastructure (Lomas, 2023). One such example is the recent "Variston" spyware campaign, which has specifically targeted Google users in the UAE (Lomas, 2023).

According to a TechCrunch report by Natasha Lomas (2023), hackers have been utilizing a sophisticated spyware called "Variston" to target Google users in the UAE. Google has actively been working to mitigate the impact of the Variston campaign and has issued a warning to users in the UAE to be vigilant about potential phishing attacks (Lomas, 2023).

The Variston spyware campaign poses significant risks to the personal data and online security of Google users in the UAE. Hackers are leveraging phishing emails and malicious links to trick users into downloading the Variston spyware onto their devices (Lomas, 2023). Once installed, the spyware can monitor users' online activities, steal sensitive information such as login credentials and financial data, and even gain control over infected devices (Lomas, 2023).

The growing prevalence of cyberattacks like the Variston campaign underscores the need for the UAE to prioritize cybersecurity and invest in robust strategies to protect its digital infrastructure (IMF, 2019). This includes working closely with the private sector and international partners, such as Google, to share information, best practices, and resources for combating cybercrime and ensuring the security of digital networks and systems (Europol, 2020).

To help safeguard their online security, individuals in the UAE should remain vigilant and take precautions to protect their personal information (Lomas, 2023). This includes using strong, unique passwords for online accounts, enabling multi-factor authentication, and being cautious about clicking on suspicious links or opening unsolicited email attachments (Lomas, 2023). Additionally, users should ensure that their devices are up-to-date with the latest security patches and antivirus software to help prevent the installation of malicious software like Variston (Lomas, 2023).

The Variston spyware campaign highlights the growing threat of cybercrime in the UAE and the need for both individuals and organizations to prioritize cybersecurity. By working together to share information and develop best practices, the UAE and its international partners can help create a more secure digital environment and protect users from the risks posed by sophisticated cyberattacks like the Variston campaign.

In conclusion, addressing organized crime in the UAE is of critical importance for the country's reputation, economic development, and the safety of its citizens. Moreover, the UAE's efforts to combat organized crime have broader implications for the international community, as they contribute to enhancing global security and stability, encourage international cooperation and information sharing, and promote sustainable development and social progress. By continuing to invest in its law enforcement capacity, strengthen its legal and regulatory frameworks, and foster international partnerships, the UAE can play a vital role in the global fight against organized crime.

In addition to the broader implications discussed above, the UAE's efforts to combat organized crime can also serve as a catalyst for change in the region, encouraging neighboring countries to adopt similar strategies and policies to address these challenges. By promoting regional collaboration and cooperation in the fight against organized crime, the UAE can help to create a safer and more secure environment for all countries in the Middle East and North Africa.

Furthermore, as a global hub for trade, finance, and innovation, the UAE can leverage its influence and resources to promote best practices and standards in the international community, fostering greater cooperation and coordination among countries and organizations in the global fight against organized crime. This can include sharing knowledge and expertise, providing technical assistance and capacity building, and supporting the development of innovative tools and technologies to detect and disrupt organized crime networks.

Ultimately, the success of the UAE's efforts to combat organized crime will depend on its ability to adapt to the rapidly evolving nature of these threats as well as its willingness to work closely with international partners and stakeholders. By staying ahead of emerging trends and challenges and fostering a culture of innovation and collaboration, the UAE can play a leading role in shaping the global response to organized crime and ensuring a safer and more secure future for all.

In the face of these challenges, the UAE has an opportunity to serve as a model for other countries, demonstrating the importance of a comprehensive and coordinated approach to combating organized crime. By investing in its law enforcement capacity, strengthening its legal and regulatory frameworks, and fostering international partnerships, the UAE can make significant progress in addressing the threats posed by organized crime and contribute to the global effort to promote safety, security, and sustainable development.

As we have seen throughout this book, the rise of organized crime, specifically the expanding influence of drug cartels and mafia networks, poses significant threats to the UAE's security, stability, and economic prosperity. These criminal organizations have woven themselves into the fabric of society, exploiting vulnerabilities in governance, technology, and the global financial system. It is now more important than ever for the UAE to take decisive action to reclaim control of the country from the clutches of these nefarious entities.

To achieve this goal, the UAE must develop and implement a comprehensive and multifaceted strategy that addresses the root causes of organized crime while simultaneously targeting the cartels and mafia networks directly. This strategy should encompass the following key components:

1. Strengthening institutions: The UAE must invest in building robust institutions that are resilient to corruption and infiltration by criminal organizations. This includes reinforcing law enforcement agencies, the judiciary, and regulatory bodies, ensuring they have the necessary resources, training, and independence to effectively combat organized crime.

2. Enhancing international cooperation: Given the transnational nature of organized crime, the UAE must actively collaborate with regional and global partners to share intelligence, resources, and best practices. This includes participating in international organizations and initiatives focused on combating organized crime, adhering to global standards for anti-money laundering, and combating the financing of terrorism.

3. Fostering public-private partnerships: The private sector plays a crucial role in combating organized crime, particularly in areas such as technology, cybersecurity, and financial services. The UAE must work closely with private sector stakeholders to develop innovative solutions, share information, and ensure that businesses are not inadvertently facilitating criminal activities.

4. Investing in technology and innovation: As criminal organizations increasingly rely on advanced technologies, the UAE must stay ahead of the curve by investing in cutting-edge tools and techniques to detect, disrupt, and dismantle these networks. This includes leveraging big data analytics, artificial intelligence, and other emerging technologies to bolster law enforcement capabilities.

5. Promoting education and awareness: To effectively combat organized crime, the UAE must ensure that its citizens are well-informed about the dangers posed by these criminal networks and the steps they can take to protect themselves and their communities. This includes investing in public awareness campaigns, educational initiatives, and community engagement programs that foster a culture of vigilance and responsibility.

By taking these bold and decisive steps, the UAE can reclaim control of its country from the grip of criminal organizations, ultimately safeguarding its security, stability, and economic well-being. The journey will not be easy, and the challenges are immense, but the UAE has the resilience, determination, and vision to rise above these adversities and build a brighter, more secure future for its people and the international community as a whole.

AFTERWORD

It is vital, as we come to the end of "Desert Shadows: Uncovering the Underworld of Drug Cartels and Mafia Networks in the UAE," to reflect on the intricacies of organized crime and the difficulties it offers to the United Arab Emirates (UAE), the region, and the globe as a whole. The purpose of this book is to provide readers with a full knowledge of the complicated web of links that exists between drug cartels and mafia groups, as well as their mode of operation and the influence that their illegal actions have on the economy, society, and global security.

Throughout the entirety of this book, we have investigated the myriad facets of this underworld, covering topics such as the utilization of cutting-edge technologies and cyber capabilities, the use of the dark web for illicit activities, and the vulnerabilities of the international monetary system. In addition, we have emphasized the essential role that international collaboration, public-private partnerships, and creative law enforcement techniques play in the fight against this diverse and always shifting danger.

When we consider the future, it is abundantly clear that the battle against organized crime, in particular the nexus that exists between drug cartels and mafia networks, will continue to be a significant obstacle to overcome. These criminal networks will continue to have access to new possibilities to extend their activities and take advantage of weaknesses in our systems due to the quick rate of technical improvements, which, when combined with the growing globalization and interconnection of our society, will continue to provide such opportunities.

However, in addition to demonstrating that there are potential solutions and strategies that can be implemented, this book has also shown that there are potential solutions and strategies that can be implemented to mitigate the impact of these criminal networks and protect the safety, stability, and security of our communities. We can work together to destroy these criminal networks and assure a brighter, more secure future for everyone if we create more international collaboration, invest in cutting-edge technology, and promote openness and accountability in our institutions. If we do this, we will be able to guarantee a better future for all of us.

You, the reader, are now armed with a more in-depth grasp of the complicated world of drug cartels and mafia networks, as well as the influence these groups have had not only on the UAE but also on other countries and regions. We have high hopes that the dissemination of this information will not only heighten people's awareness of how serious this problem is, but that it will also motivate people to take action and make a contribution to the ongoing efforts to battle organized crime in all of its guises.

As we come to the end of this discussion, it is important to keep in mind that the fight against organized crime is not solely the responsibility of law enforcement agencies, governments, or international organizations. It is a group endeavor that calls for the participation of every member of society as well as constant attention on their part. Every single one of us has the ability to play a part in making our world a safer place by remaining informed, reporting behaviors that we believe to be suspicious, and encouraging a culture of honesty and accountability.

REFERENCES

Afilipoaie, A., & Shortis, P. (2019). From drug trafficking to human trafficking: The dark web's evolving landscape. Journal of Human Trafficking, 5(2), 111-128.

Alazab, M. (2021). Cybercrime in the United Arab Emirates: An Analysis of the Legal Framework and Challenges. International Journal of Cyber Criminology, 15(1), 106-121.

Alhyas, L., Elarabi, H., & AlGhaferi, H. (2015). Adolescents' perception of substance use and factors influencing its use: a qualitative study in Abu Dhabi. JRSM Open, 6(2), 2054270414567167.

Al Jazeera. (2018). Pakistan court disqualifies PM Nawaz Sharif. Retrieved from https://www.aljazeera.com/news/2017/7/28/pakistan-court-disqualifies-pm-nawaz-sharif

Alperovitch, D., & Weidemann, M. (2017). The Need for a Cybersecurity Framework in the Gulf Cooperation Council. Retrieved from https://www.atlanticcouncil.org/in-depth-research-reports/issue-brief/the-need-for-a-cybersecurity-framework-in-the-gulf-cooperation-council/

Al Tamimi & Company. (2018). Anti-Money Laundering in the UAE: An Overview. Retrieved from https://www.tamimi.com/law-update-articles/anti-money-laundering-in-the-uae-an-overview/

AML Newsflow. (2020). Dubai: A Haven for Trade-Based Money Laundering, Says US Study. Retrieved from https://amlnewsflow.coastlinesolutions.com/2020/08/24/dubai-a-haven-for-trade-based-money-laundering-says-us-study/

Amnesty International. (2020). United Arab Emirates: Human Rights Concerns. https://www.amnesty.org/en/countries/middle-east-and-north-africa/united-arab-emirates/report-united-arab-emirates/

Baldwin-Edwards, M. (2011). Labour immigration and labour markets in the GCC countries: National patterns and trends. London School of Economics, Kuwait Programme on Development, Governance and Globalisation in the Gulf States. Retrieved from https://eprints.lse.ac.uk/55239/

Bagley, B. M. (2014). Drug trafficking, organized crime, and violence in the Americas today. University Press of Florida.

Bagley, B. M. (2014). Drug trafficking and organized crime in the Americas: Major trends in the twenty-first century. Woodrow Wilson International Center for Scholars.

BBC (2021). Interpol elects Emirati general accused of torture as president. Retrieved from https://www.bbc.com/news/world-middle-east-59419297

Bourse & Bazaar. (2021, October 27). UAE Earns Big as Iran Sells Oil to China. Retrieved from https://www.bourseandbazaar.com/articles/2021/10/27/uae-earns-big-as-iran-sells-oil-to-china

Burgis, T., & Aglionby, J. (2023). How Dubai is getting around international sanctions against Russia. The Africa Report. Retrieved from https://www.theafricareport.com/299148/how-dubai-is-getting-around-international-sanctions-against-russia/

Carnegie Endowment for International Peace. (2020, July 7). Dubai's Role in Facilitating Corruption and Global Illicit Financial Flows. Retrieved from https://carnegieendowment.org/2020/07/07/dubai-s-role-in-facilitating-corruption-and-global-illicit-financial-flows-pub-82180

Carnegie Endowment for International Peace. (2020). How Emirati Law Enforcement Allows Kleptocrats and Organized Crime to Thrive. Retrieved from https://carnegieendowment.org/2020/07/07/how-emirati-law-enforcement-allows-kleptocrats-and-organized-crime-to-thrive-pub-82187

Carpenter, A. (2016). Beyond drug wars: Transforming factional violence in Mexico. Conflict Resolution Quarterly, 33(4), 295-318.

Carrapico, H., & Farrand, B. (2017). Dialogue, partnership and empowerment for network and information security: The changing role of the private sector from regulation to enforcement. Crime, Law and Social Change, 67(3), 245-261.

Castillo, A. C., & Smith, A. (2023). The Growing Use of Cryptocurrencies by Transnational Organized Crime Groups in Latin America. Georgetown Journal of International Affairs. Retrieved from https://gjia.georgetown.edu/2023/03/20/the-growing-use-of-cryptocurrencies-by-transnational-organized-crime-groups-in-latin-america/

Chatterjee, S. (2018). Underworld 'dons' from India, Pakistan find safe haven in UAE. Khaleej Times. Retrieved from https://www.khaleejtimes.com/nation/crime/underworld-dons-from-india-pakistan-find-safe-haven-in-uae

Chaudhary, V. (2003). Dubai Doesn't Deliver, Yet Again. Outlook India. Retrieved from https://www.outlookindia.com/website/story/dubai-doesnt-deliver-yet-again/218886

Chertoff, M., & Simon, T. (2015). The Impact of the Dark Web on Internet Governance and Cyber Security. Global Commission on Internet Governance Paper Series, No. 6.

Chivers, C. J. (2008). Arms Trafficker's Vanished Empire. The New York Times. Retrieved from https://www.nytimes.com/2008/03/25/world/asia/25bout.html

Choo, K. K. R. (2021). Cryptocurrency and Money Laundering. In M. Levi & P. Reuter (Eds.), Handbook of Money Laundering and Terrorist Financing (pp. 279-301). Springer.

Cockayne, J., & Lupel, A. (2011). Rethinking the relationship between peace operations and organized crime. International Peacekeeping, 18(1), 4-20.

Cockayne, J. (2011). Transnational Organized Crime: A Growing Threat to National and International Security. United Nations University.

Connolly, P. (2020). The Kinahan Empire: How an Irish Cartel Took Over the World of International Drug Trafficking. Melville House UK.

Davidson, C. M. (2008). Dubai: The Vulnerability of Success. New York: Columbia University Press.

Detained in Dubai. (2023). Radha Stirling comments on Kaz Crossley arrest. https://detained-in-dubai.prowly.com/230169-radha-stirling-comments-on-kaz-crossley-arrest

Dollar, K. (2014). Money Laundering and Human Trafficking: The Need for Greater International Cooperation. Retrieved from https://www.gcii.org/sites/default/files/resources/ML%20and%20HT%20Policy%20Brief%20Final.pdf

Dubai Police Academy. (2021). About Us. Retrieved from https://www.dpa.gov.ae/En/Pages/About.aspx

Egmont Group. (2020). United Arab Emirates. Retrieved from https://www.egmontgroup.org/en/content/united-arab-emirates

El Universal. (2019). Mexican drug lords invest in Dubai. Retrieved from https://www.eluniversal.com.mx/english/mexican-drug-lords-invest-dubai

Europol. (2019). Drug markets report: EU Drug Markets Report 2019. Retrieved from https://www.europol.europa.eu/publications-documents/eu-drug-markets-report-2019

Europol. (2020). EU Drug Markets Report 2020. Retrieved from https://www.europol.europa.eu/activities-services/main-reports/eu-drug-markets-report-2020

Europol. (2018). Internet Organised Crime Threat Assessment 2018. Retrieved from https://www.europol.europa.eu/activities-services/main-reports/internet-organised-crime-threat-assessment-iocta-2018

Europol. (2020). Internet Organised Crime Threat Assessment 2020. Retrieved from https://www.europol.europa.eu/activities-services/main-reports/internet-organised-crime-threat-assessment-iocta-2020

Europol. (2017). Serious and Organised Crime Threat Assessment. Retrieved from https://www.europol.europa.eu/socta/2017/

Farah, D., & Braun, S. (2007). Merchant of Death: Money, Guns, Planes, and the Man Who Makes War Possible. Wiley.

FATF (2018). The financial flows that result from the trafficking of humans Retrieved from "https://www.fatf-gafi.org/media/fatf/documents/reports/Financial-flows-human-trafficking.pdf" from the website of the Financial Action Task Force (FATF).

FATF. (2020). Money Laundering and Terrorist Financing Risks and Vulnerabilities Associated with Virtual Assets. Retrieved from https://www.fatf-gafi.org/media/fatf/documents/recommendations/Virtual-Assets-FATF-Report-Guidance.pdf

FATF. (2020). Mutual Evaluation Report: United Arab Emirates. Retrieved from https://www.fatf-gafi.org/media/fatf/documents/reports/mer4/Mutual-Evaluation-Report-United-Arab-Emirates-2020.pdf

FATF. (2020). United Arab Emirates' AML/CFT Regime. Retrieved from https://www.fatf-gafi.org/publications/mutualevaluations/documents/mer-uae-2020.html

FATF (Financial Action Task Force). (2021). Virtual Assets: Red Flag Indicators of Money Laundering and Terrorist Financing. Retrieved from https://www.fatf-gafi.org/media/fatf/documents/recommendations/Virtual-Assets-Red-Flag-Indicators.pdf

Galeotti, M. (2017). Crimintern: How the Kremlin Uses Russia's Criminal Networks in Europe. European Council on Foreign Relations. Retrieved from https://www.ecfr.eu/publications/summary/crimintern_how_the_kremlin_uses_r ussias_criminal_networks_in_europe

Galeotti, M. (2017). The Vory: Russia's Super Mafia. Yale University Press.

Gangarosa, G. J. (2014). Global Crime Syndicates. In The Global Underworld: Transnational Crime and the United States (pp. 25-52). ABC-CLIO.

Gangsters Inc. (2022). Fugitive Camorra drug boss Raffaele Imperiale extradited from Dubai. Retrieved from https://gangstersinc.org/blog/fugitive-camorra-drug-boss-raffaele-imperiale-extradited-from-dub

Gardner, A. (2009). City of Extremes: The Spatial Politics of Dubai. Durham: Duke University Press.

GCC. (2017). Agreement on Mutual Legal Assistance in Criminal Matters among Gulf Cooperation Council Countries. Gulf Cooperation Council. Retrieved from https://www.gcc-sg.org/en-us/Cooperationagreements/Pages/Agreement-on-Mutual-Legal-Assistance-in-Criminal-Matters-among-Gulf-Cooperation-Council-Countries.aspx

Glenny, M. (2008). McMafia: A Journey through the Global Criminal Underworld. Vintage Books

Global Initiative Against Transnational Organized Crime. (n.d.). Balkan Criminals Find a Home in the UAE and the Gulf. Retrieved from https://globalinitiative.net/analysis/balkans-criminals-uae-gulf/

Gulf News. (2012). UAE Cybercrime Law Decree No. 5 of 2012. Retrieved from https://gulfnews.com/uae/government/uae-cybercrime-law-decree-no-5-of-2012-1.1096959

Gulf News. (2021). UAE reports surge in cybercrime cases amid COVID-19 pandemic. Retrieved from https://gulfnews.com/uae/crime/uae-reports-surge-in-cybercrime-cases-amid-covid-19-pandemic-1.1618998744622

Gupta, R., & Raghavan, S. (2020). Drug Trafficking in South Asia: A Case Study of India and Pakistan. Asian Journal of Criminology, 15(4), 201-223.

Hemaya Foundation. (2020). Hemaya Foundation. Retrieved from https://www.hemayafoundation.org

Human Rights Watch. (2006). Building Towers, Cheating Workers: Exploitation of Migrant Construction Workers in the United Arab Emirates Retrieved from https://www.hrw.org/report/2006/11/11/building-towers-cheating-workers/exploitation-migrant-construction-workers-united

Human Rights Watch. (2019). UAE: Weapons Transfers to Yemen Militias. Retrieved from https://www.hrw.org/news/2019/01/29/uae-weapons-transfers-yemen-militias

Human Rights Watch. (2021). World Report 2021: United Arab Emirates. https://www.hrw.org/world-report/2021/country-chapters/united-arab-emirates

Human Rights Watch. (2020). United Arab Emirates: Events of 2019. Retrieved from https://www.hrw.org/world-report/2020/country-chapters/united-arab-emirates

Hutchings, S., & Guala, N. (2017). Investigating the role of global transit hubs in the illicit trade of counterfeit goods. Trends in Organized Crime, 20(1-2), 77-92.

ICIJ (2022). How a Ruthless Irish Gang Found a Home Away from Home in Dubai and an Enemy in the White House. Retrieved from https://www.icij.org/inside-icij/2022/04/how-a-ruthless-irish-gang-found-a-home-away-from-home-in-dubai-and-an-enemy-in-the-white-house/

ILO. (2018). Global Estimates of Modern Slavery: Forced Labour and Forced Marriage. International Labour Organization.

IMF. (2017). United Arab Emirates: Detailed Assessment Report on Anti-Money Laundering and Combating the Financing of Terrorism. Retrieved from https://www.imf.org/en/Publications/CR/Issues/2017/05/17/United-Arab-Emirates-Detailed-Assessment-Report-on-Anti-Money-Laundering-and-Combating-the-44901

IMF. (2017). United Arab Emirates: Financial System Stability Assessment. Retrieved from https://www.imf.org/en/Publications/CR/Issues/2017/09/07/United-Arab-Emirates

IMF. (2019). Cybersecurity Risk Supervisory Guidance. https://www.imf.org/en/Publications/Policy-Papers/Issues/2019/12/09/Cybersecurity-Risk-Supervisory-Guidance-48735

IMF. (2019). Cybersecurity Risk Supervision in the Financial Sector: A Forward-Looking Approach. Retrieved from https://www.imf.org/en/Publications/Departmental-Papers-Policy-

Papers/Issues/2019/12/02/Cybersecurity-Risk-Supervision-in-the-Financial-Sector-A-Forward-Looking-Approach-48815

Inteldrop. (2023). Transnational Criminal Organizations: A Comprehensive List of the Most Notorious Groups and Their Illegal Activities. Retrieved from https://www.theinteldrop.org/2023/01/26/transnational-criminal-organizations-a-comprehensive-list-of-the-most-notorious-groups-and-their-illegal-activities/

Interpol. (2020). Cooperation Between INTERPOL and United Arab Emirates. Retrieved from https://www.interpol.int/en/Who-we-are/Member-countries/Asia-South-Pacific/UNITED-ARAB-EMIRATES

ITU. (2018). Global Cybersecurity Index (GCI) 2018. Retrieved from https://www.itu.int/dms_pub/itu-d/opb/str/D-STR-GCI.01-2018-R1-PDF-E.pdf

Jamwal, N. S. (2001). D-Company's growing influence. Jane's Intelligence Review, 13(3), 36-40.

Khan, A., & Webb, S. (2018). Trafficking of women and girls in South Asia: Prevalence, drivers, and consequences. UN Women. Retrieved from https://asiapacific.unwomen.org/en/digital-library/publications/2018/12/trafficking-of-women-and-girls-in-south-asia

Kanna, A. (2011). Dubai, the City as Corporation. Minneapolis: University of Minnesota Press.

Kaplan, E. (2008). The Capture of Viktor Bout. Council on Foreign Relations. Retrieved from https://www.cfr.org/expert-brief/capture-viktor-bout

Kaspersky Lab. (2021). Financial Cyberthreats in 2020. Retrieved from https://securelist.com/financial-cyberthreats-in-2020/100979/

Kumar, A., & Balfour, A. (2016). The United Arab Emirates: Power, Politics and Policy-Making. Routledge.

Lazarević, S. (2018). Organized Crime in the Western Balkans: Global Challenges and Local Responses. European Science, 2018(2), 71-80.

Lokhande, R. (2019). The story of Dawood Ibrahim's sprawling criminal empire. DNA India. Retrieved from https://www.dnaindia.com/india/report-d-company-in-depth-look-at-dawood-ibrahim-s-crime-syndicate-2838940

Lomas, N. (2023, March 29). Hackers use Variston spyware to target UAE Google users. TechCrunch. https://techcrunch.com/2023/03/29/hackers-variston-spyware-uae-google/

MacNamee, G. (2020). Daniel Kinahan: A controversial figure. Retrieved from https://www.rte.ie/news/2020/0615/1147365-daniel-kinahan-a-controversial-figure/

Middle East Eye. (n.d.). Dubai: How foreigners are laundering billions through UAE real estate. Retrieved from https://www.middleeasteye.net/news/uae-dubai-foreigners-laundering-billions-real-estate

Middle East Eye. (2018). UAE: Dubai foreigners laundering billions in real estate. Retrieved from https://www.middleeasteye.net/news/uae-dubai-foreigners-laundering-billions-real-estate

Middle East Eye. (2021, September 20). Dubai: UAE used by foreigners to launder billions through real estate. Retrieved from https://www.middleeasteye.net/news/uae-dubai-foreigners-laundering-billions-real-estate

Middle East Institute (MEI) (2021). Water Issues in the Gulf: Time for Action. Retrieved from https://www.mei.edu/publications/water-issues-gulf-time-action

Middle East Research and Information Project (MERIP). (2023). Illicit flows to the UAE take the shine off African gold. Retrieved from https://merip.org/2023/01/illicit-flows-to-the-uae-take-the-shine-off-african-gold-2/

Ministry of Finance UAE. (2018). UAE Cabinet Approves Law to Combat Money Laundering and Financing of Terrorism. Retrieved from https://www.mof.gov.ae/en/media/News/Pages/UAE-Cabinet-Approves-Law-to-Combat-Money-Laundering-and-Financing-of-Terrorism.aspx

Ministry of Finance. (2019). Economic Substance Regulations. Retrieved from https://www.mof.gov.ae/en/StrategicPartnerships/Pages/ESR.aspx

Morrison, J. (2018). The UAE's role in global drug trafficking networks. Global Initiative Against Transnational Organized Crime. Retrieved from https://globalinitiative.net/analysis/uae-drug-trafficking/

Nereim, V., & Algethami, S. (2018). The UAE's extraordinary rise from desert to global powerhouse. Bloomberg. Retrieved from https://www.bloomberg.com/news/features/2018-12-12/the-uae-s-extraordinary-rise-from-desert-to-global-powerhouse

Passas, N. (2005). Informal value transfer systems and criminal organizations. Journal of Money Laundering Control, 8(2), 171-183.

OCCRP. (2021). Dubai Uncovered: Data Leak Exposes How Criminals, Officials, and Sanctioned Politicians Poured Money into Dubai Real Estate. Retrieved from https://www.occrp.org/en/investigations/dubai-uncovered-data-leak-exposes-how-criminals-officials-and-sanctioned-politicians-poured-money-into-dubai-real-estate

Pravda. (2022). How UAE helps Putin's cronies avoid sanctions. Retrieved from https://www.pravda.com.ua/eng/articles/2022/03/30/7335658/

Reuters. (2012). HSBC, Standard Chartered face U.S. money laundering probe. Retrieved from https://www.reuters.com/article/us-hsbc-regulator-idUSBRE87L0S220120822

Reuter, P. (2020). The Economics of Organized Crime. Cambridge: Cambridge University Press.

Rijken, C. (2011). Combating Trafficking in Human Beings for Labour Exploitation. Intersenti

Schmidt, M. S. (2012). The Case Against Viktor Bout, an Arms Dealer, Is Not Finished Yet. The New York Times. Retrieved from https://www.nytimes.com/2012/11/12/world/case-against-viktor-bout-is-not-finished-yet.html

Serrano, M. (2018). The Sinaloa Cartel's International Reach. Retrieved from https://www.insightcrime.org/news/analysis/the-sinaloa-cartels-international-reach/

Shelley, L. I. (2014). Dirty Entanglements: Corruption, Crime, and Terrorism. Cambridge University Press.

Stirling, R. (2021). UAE bid for INTERPOL presidency: Statement from Expert Radha Stirling on Al Raisi. IPEX Reform. Retrieved from https://www.ipexreform.com/post/uae-bid-for-interpol-presidency-statement-from-expert-radha-stirling-on-al-raisi

The Borgen Project. (2020). Poverty in the United Arab Emirates. Retrieved from https://borgenproject.org/poverty-in-the-united-arab-emirates/

The Economist. (2018). The dark side of Dubai. Retrieved from https://www.economist.com/open-future/2018/08/01/the-dark-side-of-dubai

The Guardian. (2009). The dark side of Dubai: the world's favorite luxury playground. Retrieved from https://www.theguardian.com/world/2009/apr/07/dubai-property-slump-trafficking

The Guardian. (2020). Daniel Kinahan: the man behind Tyson Fury's fight with Anthony Joshua. Retrieved from https://www.theguardian.com/sport/2020/jun/11/daniel-kinahan-the-man-behind-tyson-furys-fight-with-anthony-joshua

The Irish Times. (2021). Kinahan crime group. Retrieved from https://www.irishtimes.com/topics/topics-7.1213540?article=true&tag_organisation=Kinahan+crime+group

The New Arab. (2020, December 14). Israeli criminals flee to Dubai to escape arrest. Retrieved from https://www.newarab.com/news/israeli-criminals-flee-dubai-escape-arrest

The New York Times. (2023, March 13). Dubai Emerges as a Russian Oligarch Safe Haven Amid Ukraine War. Retrieved from https://www.nytimes.com/2023/03/13/world/europe/russia-dubai-ukraine-war.html

The New York Times. (2023, April 7). South Africa's Gupta Brothers Are Back — in Dubai. Retrieved from https://www.nytimes.com/2023/04/07/world/africa/south-africa-gupta-brothers-corruption-uae-dubai.html

The Soufan Center. (2023). IntelBrief. Retrieved from https://thesoufancenter.org/intelbrief-2023-january-12/

The Hindu. (2020). UAE-based firm helped Nirav Modi launder money: ED. Retrieved from https://www.thehindu.com/news/national/uae-based-firm-helped-nirav-modi-launder-money-ed/article30774896.ece

Times of India. (2014, May 13). Dawood aide shot dead in Dubai. Times of India. Retrieved from https://timesofindia.indiatimes.com/Dawood-aide-shot-dead-in-Dubai/articleshow/34951437.cms

Transparency International. (2019). Corruption Perceptions Index 2019. Retrieved from https://www.transparency.org/en/cpi/2019/results

Transparency International. (2020). The United Arab Emirates: A key piece in the global money laundering puzzle. Retrieved from https://www.transparency.org/en/news/the-united-arab-emirates-a-key-piece-in-the-global-money-laundering-puzzle

UAE Central Bank. (2018). Anti-Money Laundering and Combating the Financing of Terrorism and Illegal Organisations Law. Retrieved from https://www.centralbank.ae/en/laws/aml-cft-law

UAE Central Bank. (2020). Regulation and Supervision. Retrieved from https://www.centralbank.ae/en/supervision/regulation

UAE Central Bank. (2020). Virtual Asset Regulation. Retrieved from https://www.centralbank.ae/en/supervision/regulatory-framework/virtual-asset-regulation

UAE Central Bank. (2021). AML/CFT Supervision. Retrieved from https://www.centralbank.ae/en/aml-cft-supervision

UAE Federal Law No. 51. (2006). Combating Human Trafficking Crimes. Retrieved from https://www.refworld.org/docid/4a6295ac2.html

UAE Government. (2020). Free zones in the UAE. Retrieved from https://u.ae/en/information-and-services/business/free-zones-in-the-uae

UAE Government. (2021). Anti-money laundering and counter-terrorist financing. Retrieved from https://u.ae/en/information-and-services/justice-safety-and-the-law/anti-money-laundering-and-counter-terrorist-financing

UAE Ministry of Education. (2018). Educational Programs. Retrieved from https://www.moe.gov.ae/En/AboutTheMinistry/Pages/EducationalPrograms.aspx

UAE Ministry of Finance. (2020). UAE Economic Substance Regulations. Retrieved from https://www.mof.gov.ae/en/strategicpartnerships/pages/esr.aspx

UAE Ministry of Foreign Affairs. (2021). UAE Foreign Aid. Retrieved from https://www.mofaic.gov.ae/en/uae-foreign-aid

UAE Ministry of Interior. (2019). Annual Report. Retrieved from https://www.moi.gov.ae/en

UAE National Cyber Security Council. (2020). About Us. Retrieved from https://www.ncsc.gov.ae/en/about

UNODC. (2016). United Arab Emirates. United Nations Office on Drugs and Crime. Retrieved from https://www.unodc.org/unodc/en/about-unodc/field-offices/unodc-office-for-the-gulf-cooperation-council-region/united-arab-emirates.html

UNODC. (2016). World Drug Report 2016. Retrieved from https://www.unodc.org/doc/wdr2016/WORLD_DRUG_REPORT_2016_web.pdf

Unger, B. (2007). The Negative Effects of Money Laundering on Economic Development. Retrieved from https://waleolusi.files.wordpress.com/2013/05/the-negative-effects-of-money-laundering-on-econom.pdf

United Nations. (2020). United Nations Convention against Transnational Organized Crime and the Protocols Thereto. Retrieved from https://www.unodc.org/unodc/en/organized-crime/intro/UNTOC.html

U.S. Department of State. (2020). 2020 International Narcotics Control Strategy Report. Retrieved from https://www.state.gov/wp-content/uploads/2020/03/Tab-1-INCSR-Vol.-I-Final-for-Printing-3-5-19.pdf

U.S. Department of State. (2020). 2020 International Narcotics Control Strategy Report (INCSR): Volume II - Money Laundering. Retrieved from https://www.state.gov/wp-content/uploads/2020/05/UAE-2020-INCSR-2-FINAL.pdf

U.S. Department of State. (2021). Trafficking in Persons Report 2021. Retrieved from https://www.state.gov/wp-content/uploads/2021/07/2021-TIP-Report-FINAL-7.1-508.pdf

U.S. Department of the Treasury. (2019). Treasury Designates Vast Iranian Petroleum Shipping Network That Supports IRGC-QF and Terror Proxies. Retrieved from https://home.treasury.gov/news/press-releases/sm789

Washington Institute. (2008). Drug Trafficking and Middle Eastern Terrorist Groups: A Growing Nexus? Retrieved from https://www.washingtoninstitute.org/policy-analysis/drug-trafficking-and-middle-eastern-terrorist-groups-growing-nexus

World Bank. (2020). The Hidden Wealth of Nations: The Scourge of Tax Havens. Retrieved from https://www.worldbank.org/en/publication/wdr2016

World Bank. (2019). The World Bank in United Arab Emirates. Retrieved from https://www.worldbank.org/en/country/gcc/overview

ABOUT THE AUTHOR

Robert Dobbs is an accomplished author, US Army Airborne veteran, and dedicated public servant with a rich background in international relations, management consulting, and education. His life experiences and academic achievements have informed his writing, which focuses on themes of resilience, leadership, and the power of personal growth.

Born and raised in Wisconsin in the United States, Robert's military career began when he enlisted in the US Army Airborne. During his service, he was deployed to several overseas locations, where he developed a strong sense of discipline and camaraderie. After completing his military duties, he transitioned into civilian life, eager to continue serving his community in other ways.

With a passion for public service, Robert spent a decade in local elected office, where he tackled various issues related to governance, social welfare, and economic development. At the same time, he was appointed to serve on a board for the Supreme Court of Wisconsin, further showcasing his dedication to the betterment of society.

Robert's keen interest in international affairs led him to spend ten years working in the Middle East and Central Asia as an education and management consultant. Here, he played an essential role in fostering understanding and cooperation between diverse cultures and organizations.

With a Master's degree in International Relations, an MBA, and a Bachelor of Science in Public Administration, Robert's education has provided him with a solid foundation for his work in both the public and private sectors. His unique combination of military, political, and international experience has given him a distinctive voice as an author, offering readers a fresh perspective on global issues and the human experience.

In his personal life, Robert is a devoted husband and father.